New Curriculum

Primary English

Learn, practise and revise

Les Ray and Gill Budgell

Year **6**

Contents

RISING STARS

Content grid

Links to English Programme of Study for Key Stage 2

	Unit title	Objective	Focus	Speak about it
1	Spelling strategies – *i* before *e*	Words with the /i/ sound spelled *ei* after c	Word reading, spelling and word structure	Terminology, purpose and links to spelling
2	Spelling strategies – derivation	Use knowledge of morphology and etymology in spelling and understand that the spelling of some words needs to be learned specifically	Word reading, spelling and word structure	Derivation and links to spelling
3	Words ending in -able and -ible	Words ending in -able and -ible	Word reading, spelling and word structure	Suffixes
4	Silent letters	Spell some words with 'silent' letters, e.g. *knight, psalm, solemn*	Word reading, spelling and word structure	Silent letters and spelling
5	Editing, proofreading	Proofread for spelling and punctuation errors; propose changes to grammar, vocabulary and punctuation to enhance effects and clarify meaning	Word reading, spelling and word structure	Terminology: homophones Process: edit and proof
6	Point of view	Plan writing by identifying the audience for and purpose of the writing, selecting the appropriate form and using other similar texts as models for their own writing	Composition and text structure	Terminology, themes, causes and points of view
7	Structures	Plan writing by identifying the audience for and purpose of the writing, selecting the appropriate form and using other similar texts as models for their own writing	Composition and text structure	Purpose and techniques
8	Test your grammar, punctuation and spelling	• Use of the passive • Using bullets to punctuate a list • Use of the semicolon • *i* before *e* • Silent letters		
9	Formal and informal	Ensure correct subject and verb agreement when using singular and plural; distinguish between the language of speech and writing and choose the appropriate register	Comprehension, composition and sentence structure	Terminology: subject, verb, singular, plural, formal, informal, dialect
10	Devices to argue and persuade	Distinguish between statements of fact and opinion	Comprehension, composition and text structure	Terminology, purpose, audience and text features
11	Cool reads	Participate in discussions about books that are read to them and those they can read for themselves, building on their own and others' ideas and challenging views courteously	Comprehension	Personal opinion and book reviews
12	Writers from different times	increase their familiarity with a wide range of books, including myths, legends and traditional stories, modern fiction, fiction from our literary heritage, and books from other cultures and traditions	Comprehension, composition and text structure	Compare treatments of text (time and place) Textual evidence
13	Writers from different places	Increase their familiarity with a wide range of books, including myths, legends and traditional stories, modern fiction, fiction from our literary heritage and books from other cultures and traditions	Comprehension, composition and sentence structure	Compare treatments of text (time and place) Textual evidence
14	Active and passive voice	Use the passive voice to affect the presentation of information in a sentence	Comprehension, composition and text structure	Terminology: active, passive, subject

	Unit title	Objective	Focus	Speak about it
15	Test your grammar, punctuation and spelling	• Expanded noun phrases • Colons • Word families • Ellipsis • Common words		
16	Narrative techniques – third person	Use brackets, dashes or commas to indicate parenthesis; propose changes to grammar, vocabulary and punctuation to enhance effects and clarify meaning	Comprehension, composition and punctuation	Terminology: exploring speech
17	Instructions: audience and purpose	Plan writing by identifying the audience for and purpose of the writing, selecting the appropriate form and using other similar texts as models for their own writing	Composition and text structure	Terminology: instructions Usage, purpose and effect
18	Biography: audience and purpose	Plan writing by identifying the audience for and purpose of the writing, selecting the appropriate form and using other similar texts as models for their own writing	Composition and text structure	Terminology: biography Usage, purpose and effect
19	Diaries: audience and purpose	Plan writing by identifying the audience for and purpose of the writing, selecting the appropriate form and using other similar texts as models for their own writing	Composition and text structure	Narration, structure and formality in relation to usage, purpose and effect
20	Ideas and supporting details	Summarise the main ideas drawn from more than one paragraph, identifying key details that support the main ideas	Comprehension, composition and text structure	Usage, purpose and effect of paragraphs
21	Argument – using sentences to persuade	Plan writing by identifying the audience for and purpose of the writing, selecting the appropriate form and using other similar texts as models for their own writing	Composition and text structure	Terminology: argument Usage, purpose and effect
22	Test your grammar, punctuation and spelling	• Cohesion across paragraphs • Elision • Using a dash rather than a comma • Words ending in -fer • Homophones		
23	Using figurative language for impact	Discuss and evaluate how authors use language, including figurative language, considering the impact on the reader	Comprehension, composition and text structure	Terminology: figurative language Usage, purpose and effect
24	Words containing -ough	Words containing the letter string -ough	Word reading, spelling and word structure	Terminology, purpose and links to spelling
25	Colons or semicolons	Use semicolons, colons or dashes to mark boundaries between independent clauses	Comprehension, composition and punctuation	Terminology: colons and semicolons Usage, purpose and effect
26	Punctuation to clarify meaning – hyphen	Use hyphens to avoid ambiguity	Comprehension, composition and punctuation	Terminology: hyphen Usage, purpose and effect
27	Revision: speech marks	Evaluate and edit by proposing changes to grammar, vocabulary and punctuation to enhance effects and clarify meaning; proofread for spelling and punctuation errors	Composition and punctuation	Terminology: inverted commas/speech marks Usage, purpose and effect
28	Test your grammar, punctuation and spelling	• Question tags • Hyphens to link words • Punctuation of speech • Words ending -ough • Useful words		

1 Spelling strategies – *i* before *e*

What strategies can you use to spell difficult words? Is learning a rule the only way? Let's investigate.

> The rule: *i* before e except after c when the sound is /ee/.
>
> There are some exceptions, such as 'seize' and 'glacier'

Word bank

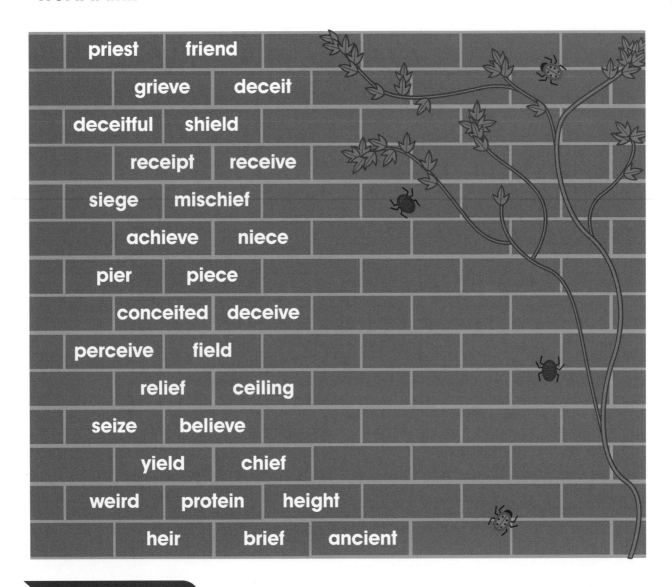

priest   friend

grieve   deceit

deceitful   shield

receipt   receive

siege   mischief

achieve   niece

pier   piece

conceited   deceive

perceive   field

relief   ceiling

seize   believe

yield   chief

weird   protein   height

heir   brief   ancient

Speak about it

What do all of these words mean?
Do they follow the rule or not?
If they do not, can you explain why?
How can you remember the exceptions to the rule?
How many different sounds does *ie* make in these words?
What tips can you give to help spell these different-sounding words?

Comprehension

1) Which word means 'in love with yourself'?

2) Which word means 'the next in line to ...'?

3) Which words are derived from the same word roots?

4) Which words are exceptions to the rule?

5) Does a dictionary give you any helpful information to explain why?

6) In which words do *ie* or *ei* make a different sound to the others?

Language focus

1) Rules are one strategy to help spelling – in this case with the sound of the word. One word in each of the following pairs is spelled incorrectly. Use the rule to find out which. Write it correctly.

   a. chief   freind   **c.** queit   priest

   b. theif   field   **d.** hieght   deceiver

2) Put *ie* or *ei* into the following words. Write them correctly.

   a. bel__ve   **c.** gr__f   **e.** conc__ve   **g.** rel__f

   b. y__ld   **d.** rec__ve   **f.** p__ce   **h.** rec__pt

3) Look closely at the letter that comes before *ie* or *ei* in the words in question 2. What is it in each case? Can you prove that the rule works?

4) How many exceptions can you find to the rule? E.g. **seize**.

Links to writing

1) One strategy to help with spelling is to look for patterns by breaking the word into syllables and pronouncing each part. Choose ten words from this unit. Break them into syllables and pronounce each one. Remember each syllable must have a vowel or a *y* sound.

2) Another strategy is to look for prefixes, suffixes or roots that you know. If you know how they work, it can make spelling easier. An etymological dictionary may help, e.g. **mis-** is a negative prefix and **re-** means **again**. Find examples of prefixes, suffixes and roots in the list of words in this unit.

3) You can always use the *look, say, cover, write, check* strategy to learn the word. Which do you find the most useful strategy and why?

2 Spelling strategies – derivation

Fred is stuck. He can't decide which are the right answers in this quiz about word derivation.

News gets its name from the first four letters of the four points of the compass – north, east, south and west. Information from all over the world.

*News from the Latin **noveles** meaning **new things**.*

Wellington named after the first Duke of Wellington. In military use in the 19th century, this was the high boot worn under the trousers.

Wellington boots to keep out the wet, invented when people had to clean out **wells**.

Alphabet named after the last two letters of the Latin alphabet. The word **alphabet** was first used by Roman children writing on their clay tablets.

*Alphabet named after the first two letters of the Latin alphabet: **alpha** and **beta** ...*

Caravan a modern word for the vehicle that is towed behind a **car** or **van**.

*Caravan from the Persian **karwan**, meaning **a group of desert travellers**. The word later came to mean a covered cart for carrying passengers and goods.*

Far-fetched means **an unlikely story**. It comes from times when storytellers roamed the land and they 'fetched' unlikely stories for people to hear.

*Far-fetched means **an unlikely story**. In the 16th century, when explorers used to return with strange things, they were known as **far-fetched goods**. They usually had a story to go with them, which people seldom believed.*

Junk was at first a name for a Javanese sailing boat, **djong**, which often transported something of little value.

*Junk from the Latin word **juncus** meaning **reed**. Rope made from this was not very good and was known as **junk rope**, as compared to the better-quality hemp rope.*

Gaffer The boss of an electrical team – he used to be in charge of the **gaff** (the place).

*Gaffer From an old English word for **grandfather**, a term of respect for someone with superior skills or someone who was your boss.*

The correct answers are in italics, like this.

> ### Speak about it
>
> Are there any words that you do not know the meaning of? If so, look them up in a dictionary.
> Does a dictionary always tell you the derivation of a word?
> What kinds of words or symbols are used to tell you where the words originated?
> Where would you look to find the derivation of a word?
> How many different countries have provided us with the words here?
> How many of the questions did you get right?
> How can the derivation of a word help you with spelling?

Comprehension

1) Which words are derived from particular words in other languages?

2) Which words are derived from ideas of what happened in the past?

3) **Wellington** is derived from someone's name. Find out which words are derived in the same way.

   a. The Scot who invented waterproof material.

   b. The earl who invented a snack out of bread.

   c. US President Roosevelt, who refused to kill large animals.

4) Are there any of these words that we do not use today?

5) How do you think these words arrived in our country, and so in our language, from so far away?

Language focus

1) How is an etymological dictionary different from the one you normally use.

2) Look at the prefixes of all these words. What do they tell you about the meaning of the words?

   a. unique   b. triangle   c. decimal   d. octet   e. biscuit

3) Find out more about the derivation of the groups of words below. From which countries did they originate?

   a. democracy, gymnasium, theatre, orchestra, telescope

   b. movie, supermarket, teenagers, detergent, gangster

   c. hamburger, dachshund, lager, kindergarten, rucksack

Links to writing

1) Investigate more words from different countries. You could link this with history work, e.g. **Which words did the Romans bring when they invaded?** (Latin and Greek) **What was the impact of the Viking invasion?** (Old Norse words, names of places) **What was the impact of the invasion of 1066?** (French words) Find examples of each of these.

2) Carry out a class survey to find out more about the derivation of your names, e.g. **Donna** is derived from the Italian for **lady**, **Neil** from the Gaelic for **champion**. Surnames often have a derivation related to an occupation. Discuss how children from different cultures may have different ways of deriving names.

3 Words ending in -able and -ible

How do you know which suffix to choose? Let's investigate!

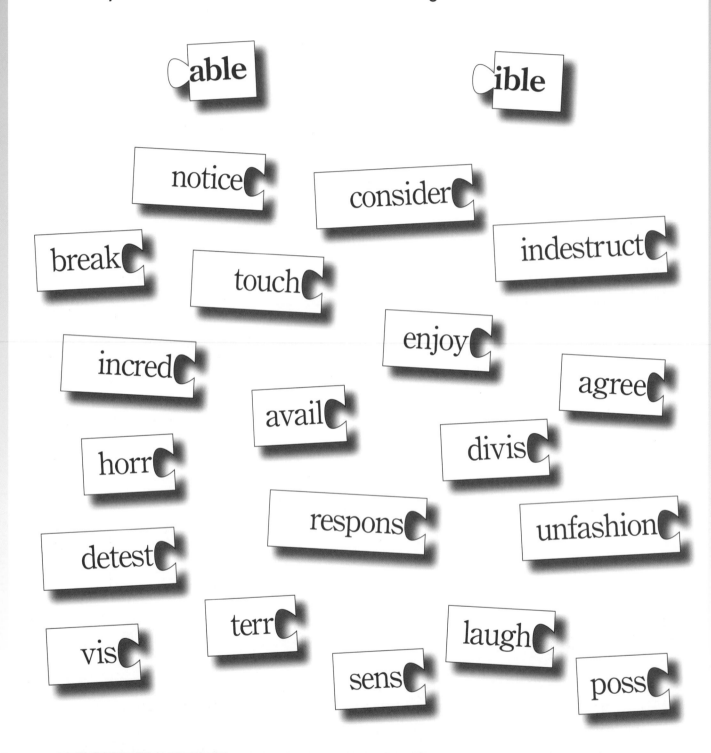

able

ible

notice

consider

break

touch

indestruct

incred

enjoy

agree

avail

divis

horr

respons

unfashion

detest

vis

terr

laugh

sens

poss

Comprehension

1) Use a dictionary to find the meaning of any words that you do not understand.

2) Which word means **can be divided**?

3) Which word means **can be broken**?

4) Which word suggests that a person is not very pleasant?

5) Which word tells you that something cannot be destroyed?

6) If you take away the suffixes, what do you notice about what you are left with?

7) List the root words of the -able examples on the opposite pages.

Language focus

1) Add **-ible** or **-able** to these root words.

   a. accept   **b.** understand   **c.** comfort   **d.** favour   **e.** laugh

2) Underline the root words of the words above. What do you notice about the root word?

3) Add **-ible** or **-able** to these words.

   a. leg   **b.** aud   **c.** invis   **d.** imposs   **e.** invinc

4) Underline the root words above. What do you notice about the root word?

5) Add **-ible** or **-able** to these words. Use a dictionary to help.

   a. rely   **b.** identify   **c.** envy   **d.** justify

   What happens to the words above?

6) Add **-ible** or **-able** to these words. Use a dictionary to help.

   a. love   **b.** forgive   **c.** excite   **d.** believe   **e.** value

   What happens to the words above?

Links to writing

1) Add **-ible** or **-able** to these words.

   a. change   **b.** knowledge   **c.** manage   **d.** like   **e.** peace

   Use a dictionary to help. What happens to the words above? Write a rule to explain it.

2) Make a poster to show ways of remembering how to spell **-ible** and **-able** words.

4 Silent letters

From *The Highwayman*

This is a part of an exciting narrative (story) poem about a highwayman in the 18th century.

The wind was a torrent of darkness among the gusty trees,

The moon was a ghostly galleon tossed upon cloudy seas.

The road was a ribbon of moonlight over the purple moor,

And the highwayman came riding—

      Riding— riding—

The highwayman came riding, up to the old inn-door.

He'd a French cocked-hat on his forehead, a bunch of lace at his chin,

A coat of the claret velvet, and breeches of brown doe-skin.

They fitted with never a wrinkle. His boots were up to the thigh.

And he rode with a jewelled twinkle,

      His pistol butts a-twinkle,

His rapier hilt a-twinkle, under the jewelled sky.

Over the cobbles he clattered and clashed in the dark inn-yard.

And he tapped with his whip on the shutters, but all was locked and barred.

He whistled a tune to the window, and who should be waiting there

But the landlord's black-eyed daughter,

      Bess, the landlord's daughter,

Plaiting a dark red love-knot into her long black hair.

Alfred Noyes

Speak about it

In words with silent letters, the silent letters are not pronounced, e.g. **knight**
The *k* is a silent letter. What spellings have you identified with silent letters?
How do they cause problems with spelling? Give some examples.
Are there any words that cause you particular problems?
How can you learn to spell them more easily?

Comprehension

1) What was the weather like? How does this add to the atmosphere of the poem?

2) What details about clothing tell you the poem is based in another time?

3) How does the poet communicate sounds to you? Quote some interesting words that he uses.

4) Does the poet think that Bess is attractive? Give your reasons.

5) What do you think will happen next in the story? Why?

Language focus

1) Find four words in the passage containing silent letters.

2) Think of other words with the same silent letters. 'Ghostly' contains a silent *h*. Another word like it would be 'Christmas'.

3) Put these words into six different groups in a chart and add two more words to each group.

badge   bridge   castle   climb   debt   doubt   hymn   knuckle listening   muscle   plumber scent   science   subtle   wrinkled   writer

Silent ... d	k	t	b	n	c	w

4) Investigate the letters before and after the silent letters. See if any patterns emerge.

5) Write rules for spelling words containing each of the silent letters above, e.g. **a silent *k* normally comes before *n*.**

Links to writing

1) Write some amusing statements containing as many words with silent letters as possible. Swap them with a friend to see if they can add any more.

   I saw the ghostly pharaoh. He had been embalmed – wrapped in ghastly bandages. He was sighing near his tomb.

2) Many words with silent letters seem to create a mysterious atmosphere from the past, e.g. **knight   castle   pharaoh   tomb   ghost   embalmed**

   What impression do they create? Use these words to write such a story.

3) Publish your story using the computer and check the spelling of the words with silent letters.

5 Editing, proofreading

Poet Tree With Mist Aches

I have a spelling chequer
It came with my pea sea
It plainly marques four my revue
Miss steaks eye cannot sea.

Eye strike a quay and right a word
And weight four it two say
Weather eye am wrong oar write
It shows me strait away.

As soon as a mist ache is maid
It nose bee fore to late
And eye can putt the error rite
It's rarely, rarely great.

I've run this poem threw it
I'm shore your pleased too no
It's letter perfect in its weigh
My chequer tolled me sew.

Sauce unknown

Speak about it

What is the poet using to write the poem?
What do you notice about the spelling in the poem?
What point is the poet trying to make?
How many of the spellings can you correct?
Why is the poem amusing?

Comprehension

1) A good way to edit and proofread is by using a highlighter. Photocopy the poem and mark any words that are incorrect.

2) Beside them, write the correct version of the words, if you know them.

3) Check your answers in your dictionary. You could look up any words that you do not know.

4) Take a verse. Put in some punctuation at the end of the lines. What would be the best to use? Compare your version with someone else and talk about the differences.

5) Write a correctly spelled version of the poem using your computer. Take care with the spellchecker!

Language focus

1) Homophones are words that sound the same but have different meanings and are spelled differently. Find ten examples in the poem.

2) Use a dictionary to find the meanings of these words in the poem.
   a. marques **b.** quay **c.** putt **d.** rite **e.** tolled

3) Find other spellings for words that sound like:
   a. ate **c.** steel **e.** two **g.** heir **i.** cereal
   b. sore **d.** tail **f.** there **h.** practise **j.** stationary

4) Find out more about homophones, homonyms and homographs. What is the difference between them? Use the Internet to research.

Links to writing

1) Write a list of helpful hints to someone who is just about to use a computer spellchecker, so that they avoid these problems.

2) Edit and present this in the most appropriate way. Print and display in the classroom.

3) You could present what you have found out about these strange words to the rest of the class. Make a PowerPoint presentation in a group.

4) Tell an amusing story based on a misunderstanding in spelling caused by a computer spellchecker.

6 Point of view

Look at the picture of the accident. How would the different people tell the story?

When you are writing, you need to have a clear idea about who you are writing for and what the purpose is. Some examples are in the table.

Audience	Purpose
parents	entertain
teenagers	persuade
children in your class	inform
head teacher	explain
nursery children	recount

Speak about it

Who is involved directly in the accident?

How would they want to tell people about what happened?

For each of the points of view, if they had to write what they saw, who might their audience be?

What would be the purpose of their writing?

Would each account be similar or different? Why

Comprehension

1) Describe what each person might see at the accident.

2) Is this influenced by where the person is positioned?

3) What other senses would be involved? What could each person say about these?

4) How much of each person's account can you believe as 'the whole truth'?

5) How will each point of view appeal to a different audience and therefore require a different style? Which versions will use the first person, the third person, the present tense, the past tense?

Language focus

1) You are the police officer at the scene. Write what would be in your notebook describing the scene. Why is your statement written in this style? Is it factual?

2) You are the car driver (Mr Roberts). Tell the story of your day to your sister in conversation as she visits you in hospital. How is this different from the style of the police officer?

3) You are one of the firefighters. Tell your version of the incident. What style will your report be written in?

4) You are the newspaper reporter. Write the newspaper article that appears that evening in the local newspaper. Is it factual?

5) You are Mrs Roberts. Tell the story of how your husband's accident changed your day. Which facts would you choose to include?

Links to writing

1) Choose a newspaper article – it could be a sports review. Rewrite the news story from a completely different point of view.

   Whose point of view will you choose?

   What do the people in the article see, hear, feel?

   How will it be different from the original?

2) Imagine that you are transformed into an animal for a day, e.g. a **cat**. Write about your adventures.

   What will the world be like for you?

   What is the world like to the animal – big, small, microscopic?

   How does the animal deal with its surroundings?

7 Structures

My East End

My part of East London has a character all its own. There is a collection of streets, parallel to each other, leading back from the old railway line. The crumbling terraced houses are full of life, even if they look old. Above them are the Docklands Light Railway lines. Huge concrete pillars hold up these tracks. They remind me of enormous grey legs striding across the city. The driverless trains on them are like blue caterpillars crawling slowly on their way to find somewhere to rest underneath the railway arches.

These arches make a new little world. In between the pillars, the spaces have been cleverly used. Some spaces have been bricked in and walls divide them into workshops or dark offices. Each space is a secret place and each one is different. One is a workshop, one is a garage – some are just mysterious.

One of the arches has been blocked off by old advertising boards, so from the train you could read about drinks or shampoo or banks. It was obviously empty and had been so for some time. This is what made me interested. Maybe this was just the home our gang needed.

Speak about it

What is being described in each paragraph?

How is each paragraph very different in what it describes?

How does one paragraph link to another?

Why has the text been put into the shape that it has?

What do you think might be in the next paragraph, if there was one?

Why do you think we talk about these paragraphs forming a **structure**?

Comprehension

1) What does the first paragraph describe?

2) Find its topic sentence and the sentences that illustrate it.

3) What do the other two paragraphs describe?

4) Show how what is described keeps becoming smaller.

5) How do you know that this is a story and not an autobiography?

Language focus

1) Continue with this story. Use the same paragraph structure – start large and get smaller.

   Describe the arch from the outside and what the gang will do with it.

   Go inside the arch and describe it.

   Focus on a person in the room.

   Use speech to say more about this person.

2) How and why is speech set out in paragraphs? What happens if it is not?

Links to writing

1) In this description, the writer starts looking from a wide angle and then focuses in on something smaller. Write a three-paragraph description of your school following the same plan.

   In the first paragraph, describe the whole area and its features.

   In the second paragraph, describe one part of this area.

   In the third paragraph, describe one smaller thing in this part.

   Use detail that will show you really know the area.

2) Edit your description to write the opening of a story about something really terrible that happens at your school. Like a film, have the long shot, medium shot and close-up happening within seconds for maximum effect.

3) Find or take photographs of your area, and the parts of your area, to illustrate your writing.

8 Test your grammar, punctuation and spelling

Grammar

Use of the passive

Write out 1–8. Write **A** if the sentence is active and **P** if it is passive.

1) The children organised the charity cake stall.

2) The date was set.

3) The cakes were provided by Mr Thomas.

4) In total, £150 was donated to the chosen charity.

5) The charity provides food for the homeless.

6) The food parcels were delivered within a week.

7) The parcels were appreciated.

8) The children planned another event as it had been such a success.

Punctuation

Using bullets to punctuate a list

Write out each block of information with a hyphen, correct punctuation and as a bulleted list.

items to take with you

sunscreen

swimming trunks or costume

towel

hat

what is the best sun protection

Tshirt

wetsuit

sunscreen

sun umbrella

surfers need to have

a surfboard

a wetsuit

goggles

a whistle

Use of the semicolon

Write an ending for each sentence, making sure that there is a complete sentence after the semicolon.

1) Tom liked going to the club;

2) Anna went home early;

3) Seeing friends is good for you;

4) Getting enough sleep is important;

5) Playing sport helps to keep you healthy;

6) Reading at night can help you sleep;

Spelling

i before *e*

Write out the rule for spelling words with *i* and *e* after *c*.

Write the correct spelling of these words.

1) deceive or decieve

2) receive or recieve

3) reciept or receipt

4) protien or protein

5) ceiling or cieling

6) seize or sieze

7) deceit or deciet

Which two are exceptions to the rule?

Silent letters

Copy and complete the chart. From your examples, write a rule to help spell words containing silent letters.

	Examples of words	Rule
silent **k**		
silent **t**		
silent **g**		
silent **b**		
silent **n**		
Another example of your choice		

9 Formal and informal

From *The Adventures of Huckleberry Finn*

Huckleberry Finn lives in America in the 19th century.
He loves being free to play by the river, but his
nasty father is trying to stop him. In this extract he
describes how he hopes to escape without trace.
He writes very much as he speaks and does not bother much about grammar.

While we laid off after breakfast to sleep up, both of us being about wore out, I got to thinking that if I could fix up some way to keep pap and the widow from trying to follow me, it would be a certainer thing than trusting to luck to get far enough off before they missed me; you see, all kinds of things might happen. Well, I didn't see no way for a while, but by and by pap raised up a minute, to drink another barrel of water, and he says: 'Another time a man comes a-prowling round here you roust me out, you hear? That man warn't here for no good. I'd a shot him. Next time, you roust me out, you hear?'

Then he dropped down and went to sleep again; but what he had been saying give me the very idea I wanted. I says to myself, I can fix it now so nobody won't think of following me.

About twelve o'clock we turned out and went along up the bank. The river was coming up pretty fast, and lots of driftwood going by on the rise. By and by along comes a log raft – nine logs fast together. We went out with the skiff and towed it ashore. Then we had dinner. Anybody but pap would a waited and seen the day through, so as to catch more stuff; but that warn't pap's style. Nine logs was enough for one time; he must shove right over to town and sell. So he locked me in and took the skiff, and started off towing the raft about half-past three. I judged he wouldn't come back that night. I waited till I reckoned he had got a good start; then I out with my saw, and went to work on that log again. Before he was t'other side of the river I was out of the hole ....

Mark Twain

Speak about it

Which words can you recognise as **spoken** or **informal** language?
Is the passage easy to understand?
Would it have been easier if it had been written in more formal English?
When you talk to a friend in the playground, how is this different from when you talk to a teacher?
Do you expect someone who lives and has been brought up in a different part of the country to speak differently from you?
What is a dialect? Does the area you live in have a particular dialect? Give some examples of special words, and give a 'translation'.

Comprehension

1) How do we know that the river that they live by is a large one?

2) How do we know that this story is set in the past?

3) How did Huck's father make a living?

4) What sort of man is Huck's father? What does his reaction to the stranger prove to us?

5) What is Huck's plan after his father had left for town? How does he go about it?

6) Identify three words or phrases that tell us immediately that Huck is speaking to us in his own words.

Language focus

1) Explain why the following are **informal** English and how they do not use proper English grammar. Correct them.

   a. both of us being about wore out

   b. if I could fix up some way to keep pap and the widow from trying to follow me

   c. it would be a certainer thing

   d. Well, I didn't see no way for a while

   e. That man warn't here for no good. I'd a shot him.

   f. but what he had been saying give me the very idea

2) Rewrite the following in **formal** English. Explain why you have changed things.

   a. but what he had been saying give me the very idea I wanted.

   b. I says to myself, I can fix it now

   c. I can fix it now so nobody won't think of following me

   d. Anybody but pap would a waited

   e. but that warn't pap's style.

   f. Nine logs was enough for one time

   g. then I out with my saw and went to work

3) Which do you think is the best style for the story of Huck Finn – formal or informal English? Explain why.

Links to writing

1) What does this passage tell us about the kind of person Huck is?

   What does he do and say?

   How does he react to other people?

2) Write the opening paragraphs of the story in formal English now, using correct grammar.

10 Devices to argue and persuade

Adapted from *Shooting the Elephant*

Nearly all sports practised nowadays are competitive. You play to win, and the game has little meaning unless you do your utmost to win. On the village green, where you pick up sides and no feeling of local patriotism is involved, it is possible to play simply for the fun and exercise: but as soon as the question of prestige arises, as soon as you feel some larger unit will be disgraced if you lose, are not the most savage combative instincts aroused? Anyone who has played in a school football match knows this. At the international level, sport is frankly mimic warfare. But the significant thing is not the behaviour of the players but the attitude of the spectators, of the nations who work themselves into furies over these absurd contests …

As soon as strong feelings of rivalry are aroused, the notion of playing the game according to the rules always vanishes. People want to see one side on top and the other side humiliated, and they forget that victory gained through cheating or through the intervention of the crowd is meaningless. Even when the spectators don't intervene physically don't they try to influence the game by cheering their own side and 'rattling' opposing players with boos and insults? Serious sport has nothing to do with fair play. It is bound up with hatred, jealousy, boastfulness, disregard of all rules and sadistic pleasure in witnessing violence: in other words, it is war minus the shooting.

George Orwell

Speak about it

What does the writer say is different between playing sport 'on the village green' and in a 'school football match'?

Do you think the writer approves of competitive sport? Why?

Do you agree with the writer's argument about sport?

Do you think there is a solution to the problem he talks about? If so what is it?

How do you know that the writer is trying to persuade you of his argument?

How much of what the author says is fact? How much is his opinion? How do you know?

Comprehension

1) Why do people play competitive sport?

2) What sort of attitudes does the author say it creates?

3) Are these attitudes good or bad? Can you think of any examples from when you have played or watched sport when things like this have happened? Give some examples and explain why you think these things happened.

4) Who does the writer blame for this attitude: the players or the spectators?

5) What examples does the author give to prove that these people make things worse?

Language focus

1) Find examples of the author using **you** in the passage. Is this direct appeal to the reader more persuasive than using **I**?

2) Writers of arguments also like to group people together to suggest that **everyone** believes the same as he or she does. This is called using **generalisation**, and is a persuasive writing technique. Can you find examples of this in the passage?

3) Look at the way the writer starts some sentences in the argument: 'Even when … '
How do these words help to make the argument flow better?

4) Rhetorical questions are a special kind of question which, although they are 'asked', actually require no answer. We use them when we are trying to be persuasive.
Find examples in the passage. How do you think they help in persuading you?
How much do they involve you in the argument?

Links to writing

1) Write two paragraphs to argue that competitive sport is a good thing. Use the persuasive techniques that this unit shows.
Choose information to back up your arguments.
Create a personal relationship with the reader, sometimes by using you**, in order to include them.**
Use statements or rhetorical questions to suggest that certain facts are absolutely correct.
Use words such as people **and** everyone **to suggest that we all believe the argument.**
Choose connectives carefully to link ideas logically: therefore … however … moreover … **and to develop the argument.**

11 Cool reads

This review is by Rick Barnes from London. He wrote this review when he was 12 years old.

Stormbreaker (Alex Rider Adventures Book 1)

by Anthony Horowitz

Walker Books, 2005, 256 pages, ISBN 978 1 844 28092 6

How easy was it to get stuck into this book?

I love the book. It's action-packed and keeps you on the edge of your seat. Horowitz outdid himself in this James Bond-like thriller. It is full of action and mystery and a bit of humour. Some kids might find it a bit violent, but I didn't. The exciting plot and the kid-spy theme is new, too. I like the gory description, but it might limit the writer's possible audience.

Who are the main characters?

Alex is resourceful. He always risks his life for others. His gadgets are always priceless! Alex is an amazing role model for kids. The book really is kind of educational, because in each book, there's lots of science. Billionaire Herod Sayle is the baddie. He is giving computers to every school in England. But MI6 is suspicious of his motives, and Uncle Ian was killed while investigating him.

What's the storyline?

Alex Rider has lived with his Uncle Ian since his parents were killed in an accident. Ian dies in an accident as well. Alex investigates and finds that his uncle was a spy for Britain's MI6, and his death was no accident. Now MI6 wants Alex to spy for them as well, though he is only 14.

How is it written?

This is like a Bond movie for kids – just for fun. Full of action, suspense, thrill-a-minute adventure, gadgets, and one boy who saves the world through brains, guts, and martial arts, it will keep readers enthralled.

Other books by the same author?

There is a complete series – all great! Read Point Blank and Skeleton Key.

The overall verdict is ... ★★★★★ !

Speak about it

Why is Rick writing about this book?

Who is his audience? What is he trying to achieve?

What does he like about the book?

Does he see any drawbacks to it?

What do you notice about the way that the review has been written on the page?

Does this make it easier or more difficult to read? Explain why.

Comprehension

1) Why do book reviews contain information such as the name of the publisher and the year of publication?

2) What kind of book is this? What other kinds of books is it like?

3) What does the writer like a lot about the book?

4) What does the writer tell you about Alex?

5) Who is the villain? What is he trying to do?

6) Is there anything people might not like about this book?

7) What is the biggest attraction to the writer about the way the book is written?

Language focus

1) The book review comes from the Internet and has not been edited. Rewrite it, paying more attention to full stops and commas.

2) Check your new version with a friend. Do they use the same punctuation?

3) Rewrite the following, explaining what the writer really meant.

   a. It's action-packed and keeps you on the edge of your seat.
   b. … the kid-spy theme is new, too.
   c. This is like a Bond movie for kids.

4) The review has a particular structure. List the headings. Which other headings would you add to make the review better, e.g.:

   Things I didn't like about this book
   Would I recommend it to a friend?

Links to writing

1) Using the structure identified above, write a book review.
   Use the same amount of text and information as Rick Barnes's review.
   Use the same kind of language.
   Set out your review using a computer: use fonts, spacing and other layout features to make the information clear.

2) Keep a reading journal for a few weeks.
   Give important details about each book you read or look at for research.
   Explain why you found it interesting or useful.
   Which examples will you use to prove your points?

12 Writers from different times

Help! Fred has to read some of Shakespeare's
Romeo and Juliet in class!
He has found two versions.

Nurse: Madam, your mother craves a word with you.

Romeo: What is her mother?

Nurse: Marry bachelor.
Her mother is the lady of the house,
And a good lady, and a wise and virtuous …

Romeo: Is she a Capulet?
O dear account! My life is my foe's debt.

(Exeunt all but Juliet and the Nurse)

Juliet: Come hither Nurse. What is yond gentleman? … What's he that follows there, that would not dance?

Nurse: I know not.

Juliet: Go ask his name. If he be married,
My grave is like to be my wedding bed.

Nurse: His name is Romeo, and a Montague;
The only son of your great enemy.

Juliet: My only love sprung from my only hate!

Speak about it

Which version do you think is easier to understand? Why?

Which words in the original do you not understand?

In which period of history was Shakespeare writing?

How could you find out the meaning of the difficult words?

Do you know the rest of the story? How does it end?

Besides the language, what other things might make writers from the past difficult to read and understand?

Look at another scene in Shakespeare's *Romeo and Juliet* to find the words he used.

How much of that scene do you understand? What can you use to help you?

Comprehension

1) In the cartoon version of the play, how can you tell who the characters are?

2) Who is the hero and who is the heroine of this story? How do you know?

3) In the cartoon, how do the pictures give you information besides the words the characters speak?

4) Does the cartoon use the same words as Shakespeare's original? What is left out?

5) In the playscript, how does Shakespeare tell you who is on stage?

6) How does Shakespeare tell the actors how to behave?

7) Can the playscript features be used in the cartoon version? Explain your answer.

Language focus

1) Shakespeare wrote this in the 1590s. Language has changed since then. How would we say the following today?

    a. '… your mother craves a word with you.'

    b. 'Her mother is the lady of the house.'

    c. 'Come hither Nurse.'

    d. 'What is yond gentleman?'

2) Other words that we use have changed their original meaning. Find out what these words used to mean in the past.

    a. nice   **b.** villain   **c.** awful   **d.** horrid   **e.** naughty

You may need to use an etymological dictionary or the Internet.

Links to writing

1) Find out more about the story of *Romeo and Juliet*. Choose one episode from it and produce it as a one-page cartoon story for people of your own age.

When you draw it, what clothes will they be wearing?

Where is the story set? This will determine the background of your pictures.

What words will you give the characters to say?

Will you use the language of the time?

13 Writers from different places

From *Little House in the Big Woods*

Laura and Mary had never seen a town. They had never seen a store. They had never seen even two houses standing together. But they knew that in a town there were many houses, and a store full of candy and calico and other wonderful things – powder, and shot, and salt, and store sugar.

They knew that Pa would trade his furs to the storekeeper for beautiful things from town, and all day they were expecting the presents he would bring them. When the sun sank low above the treetops and no more drops fell from the tips of the icicles they began to watch eagerly for Pa.

The sun sank out of sight, the woods grew dark, and he did not come. Ma started supper and set the table, but he did not come. It was time to do the chores, and still he had not come.

Ma said that Laura might come with her while she milked the cow. Laura could carry the lantern.

So Laura put on her coat and Ma buttoned it up. And Laura put her hands into the red mittens that hung by a red yarn string around her neck, while Ma lighted the candle in the lantern.

Laura was proud to be helping Ma with the milking, and she carried the lantern very carefully. Its sides were of tin, with places cut in them for the candle-light to shine through.

When Laura walked behind Ma on the path to the barn, the little bits of candle-light from the lantern leaped all around her on the snow. The night was not yet quite dark. The woods were dark, but there was a grey light on the snowy path, and in the sky there were a few faint stars. The stars did not look as warm and bright as the little lights that came from the lantern.

Laura was surprised to see the dark shape of Sukey, the brown cow, standing at the barnyard gate. Ma was surprised, too.

It was too early in the spring for Sukey to be let out in the Big Woods to eat grass. She lived in the barn. But sometimes on warm days Pa left the door of her stall open so she could come into the barnyard. Now Ma and Laura saw her behind the bars, waiting for them.

Laura Ingalls Wilder

Speak about it

How do you know that this is probably set in another place, very different from where you live?

What kinds of things do the children have or not have?

How are these different from your experience?

What tells you that the story is also probably set in the past?

Are there any words that tell you this might be written by someone from another country?

What do you find unusual about how the children behave?

Comprehension

1) The children had never seen two houses standing together. What could this tell you about the kind of place they lived in?

2) What kind of things did the children know were in town?

3) What did the children's father do in the store?

4) What detail in the passage tells you about the season?

5) What kind of chores did the girls do?

6) Why were Ma and Laura surprised to see Sukey at the gate?

Language focus

1) The story is set in the pioneering days of the United States, in the Midwest during the mid-19th century. Research detail to create a sense of another place. You can make your writing more effective by concentrating on:
   - **the words that are spoken**
   - **the comments you use to say how they are spoken**
   - **the detail of the scene around you**
   - **the events and places that they talk about.**

2) Imagine that the girls go to town. Write about their first visit to a town.
   What do they see – the buildings, the streets, the people, their behaviour?
   What did they feel about it?
   How will you make the place come alive for your reader?

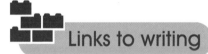

Links to writing

1) Plan another story set in the Midwest. You could use the same characters and include some kind of problem or crisis.

Once you have decided on your plot, write your story so that your reader finds out about details of life in the Midwest through the action or descriptions in the story, e.g.:
   - **daily life**
   - **food and clothes**
   - **ways of talking (any special words used).**

Remember not to write descriptions of these points. You are not writing an account of life in the Midwest. You must give the reader a strong impression of the place as you tell the story.

14 Active and passive voice

Read this account of a science experiment. This is an information text.
Its purpose is to give a lot of accurate information in a few lines.

The test tube was taken by the teacher and was placed in the flame. It was then heated until some bubbles in the water were seen. The temperature of the liquid was taken and recorded in a chart. Then the liquid was left in a cold place until it was seen to change colour. While this was happening, the white solid was heated in another part of the room. When this was seen to change colour and to give off a gas, the liquid and the solid were mixed together. Small blue crystals were seen to form.

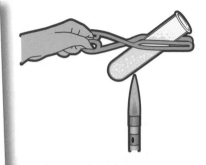

The verbs are said to be in the passive voice because the thing or person that does the acting is not mentioned. Something is being done to the subject of the sentence.

Look at the following phrases.

'The test tube **was taken** ... the white solid **was heated** ...'

The important information is about the process. The reader does not need to know who is doing the action. He or she needs to know the facts. Notice the difference with the active voice.

'I **took** the test tube and placed it in the flame ...
We **heated** the white solid in another part of the room.'

The verbs are said to be in the active voice because the subject of the sentence is actually performing the action.

Reasons for using the passive

It is appropriate to the purpose of the writing, e.g. a science experiment.
You may not know who is performing the action, e.g. My bike was stolen.
You may not wish to mention it, e.g. The vase got broken, Mum.
It may be more polite, e.g. Actually, I wasn't told about the new ticket so I should not have to pay.

Speak about it

Why is it important to use the appropriate style for certain kinds of writing?
Why do people use the active or the passive voice in writing?
What is the **subject** of a sentence?
How can you identify whether a verb is being used in the active or the passive voice?
When do you use these two different kinds of verb in your writing at school?

Comprehension

1) What is this purpose of the information text? Why does it not need to have 'a personal touch'?

2) In the passive voice, what kind of words do you notice being used with the verb?

3) Explain how the active voice differs from the passive? How can you identify which is being used by looking for the subject of the sentence?

4) What does 'the important information is about the process 'mean?

5) State three other uses for the passive voice in writing.

Language focus

1) Copy the sentences. Underline the verbs. Change the passive verb to an active one.

   a. My rucksack is being inspected by the customs officer.

   b. The store doors are guarded by two huge guards.

   c. I was shown to my seat by a guide.

   d. In our class, children are helped by two assistants.

   e. The ancient Egyptian pot was dropped by the curator.

2) Make these active sentences passive.

   a. The vicar drove the car. The car …

   b. New technology directs the police directly to the scene of the crime. The police …

   c. In the skyscraper, glass lifts take customers to the top. Customers …

   d. Our garages carry out all kinds of van repairs. All kinds …

   e. Thick fog delayed the departure of our plane. Our plane …

Links to writing

1) Rewrite the experiment on the opposite page using only active verbs. What difference does it make?

2) Explanations, e.g. for how to play a game, are often written in the passive voice, e.g.:

one person is chosen to come up with a list of words … the game must be played by ….

Write an explanation of how to play one of your favourite games. Use the passive voice where appropriate. Rewrite it using the active voice, e.g.:

You should choose a person … six people can play this game …

What differences do you notice? Which is best for the audience and the purpose of the writing?

15 Test your grammar, punctuation and spelling

Grammar

Expanded noun phrases

Use the words in the chart to write five expanded noun phrases. e.g. **A very loud steel drum echoed.**

Determiner	Adverb	Adjective	Noun	Main noun (You may add s)	Verb
A	slightly	fierce	sausage	roll	danced
That	extremely	small	steel	dog	barked
Some	very	loud	blood	drum	sneezed
Several	horrifically	pink	computer	hound	ripped
The		terrifying		bag	echoed

Punctuation

Ellipsis

Copy out the chart and tick to show why an ellipsis has been used.

	To show that a speaker didn't finish	To show a pause	To show words missed out
'I was just thinking … , ' murmured the girl.			
The policeman said, ' … he had been caught for a similar offence before.'			
Maya sat and watched … and watched … and watched.			
'Hey … you … can you … hear … me?' yelled Ben.			
The report said that in the great scheme of things … the expedition had gone well.			
'Turn to the right … no, to the left … no, the other way!' shouted Dan.			

RISING STARS

English Study Guide: Year 6

Answer Booklet

1 Spelling strategies – *i before e*
Comprehension
1) conceited
2) heir
3) grieve, achieve, perceive, receive, deceive, believe
4) seize, weird, protein, height, heir
5) *Own answer*
6) friend, heir, height

Language focus
1) a. friend
   b. thief
   c. quiet
   d. height
2) a. believe
   b. yield
   c. grief
   d. receive
   e. conceive
   f. piece
   g. relief
   h. receipt
3) *l* before *ie* in *believe*
   y before *ie* in *yield*
   r before *ie* in *grief*
   c before *ei* in *receive*
   c before *ei* in *conceive*
   p before *ie* in *piece*
   i before *ie* in *relief*
   c before *ei* in *receipt*
   The rule does work.
4) *Own answer*

Links to writing
1) re-lief
   de-ceit-ful
   brief
   pro-tein
   yield
   re-ceive
   piece
   niece
   heir
   siege
2) mischief
   deceit
   deceitful
   deceive
   receipt
   receive
3) *Own answer*

2 Spelling strategies – derivation
Comprehension
1) news
   alphabet
   caravan
   junk
   gaffer (**Old** English)
2) wellington
   far-fetched
3) a. macintosh b. sandwich c. teddy
4) no
5) People travelled around the world visiting other countries, selling and trading goods. They took their language with them.

Language focus
1) An etymological dictionary explains the origin of words as well as their meanings.
2) a. *uni-* from the Latin *unicus* meaning 'one', **unique** means 'being the only one'.
   b. *tri-* from Latin and Greek meaning 'three'; **triangle** means 'a polygon having three sides'.

c. *deci-* from Latin meaning 'tithe' or 10; **decimal** means 'based on the number 10'.
d. *oct-* from Latin meaning 'eight'; **octet** means 'a group or set of eight'.
e. *bi-* from Latin meaning 'two'; **biscuit** means 'twice baked'.
3) a. Greece b. America c. Germany

Links to writing
1), 2) *Own answers*

3 Words ending in -able and -ible
Comprehension
1) *Own answer*
2) divisible
3) breakable
4) detestable, horrible
5) indestructible
6) If you take the **-ible** suffix away, the words don't make sense. If you take the **-able** suffix away, the words do make sense.
7) agree, avail, break, consider, detest, enjoy, laugh, notice, touch, (un)fashion

Language focus
1) a. acceptable
   b. understandable
   c. comfortable
   d. favourable
   e. laughable
2) The root words all make sense.
3) a. legible
   b. audible
   c. invisible
   d. impossible
   e. invincible
4) The roots words don't make sense.
5) a. reliable
   b. identifiable
   c. enviable
   d. justifiable
   The -y is replaced with an -i before the suffix is added.
6) a. lovable
   b. forgivable
   c. excitable
   d. believable
   e. valuable
   Remove the -e before adding the suffix.

Links to writing
1) a. changeable
   b. knowledgeable
   c. manageable
   d. likeable
   e. peaceable
   Keep the -e before adding the suffix to keep the g or k sounding soft
2) *Own answer*

4 Silent letters
Comprehension
1) The weather is stormy: '*gusty*', '*tossed*', '*cloudy*'. It adds to the mystery.
2) '*French cocked-hat*', '*bunch of lace at his chin*', '*breeches of brown doe-skin*'.
3) The poet uses onomatopoeia – words that make the sound they are describing, e.g. '*clattered and clashed*'.
4) Bess has her beautiful features described in detail: '*black-eyed*', '*long black hair*'.
5) *Own answers*

Language focus
1) '*ghostly*', '*wrinkle*', '*whip*', '*whistled*'
2) Examples include: silent *h* – hour, hurrah, khaki, heir, exhaust, Thames, exhibition
   silent *w* – sword, answer, Norwich, write, two, wrist, writ, whole

3)

Silent ...	
d	badge, bridge
k	knuckle
t	castle, listening
b	climb, debt, doubt, plumber, subtle
n	hymn
c	muscle, scent, science
w	writer, wrinkled

4) Letters before and after. Examples include: silent *g* normally comes before an *n* – gnome, design. Silent *u* normally comes before a *g* – guard, guess. Silent *h* often after a *w* – why, whether. Silent *k* often before *n* – knight, knuckle. Silent *b* often at the end of a word – climb, thumb or before a *t* – debt. Silent *l* often before a *k* or *m* – yolk, palm. Silent *w* often before *r* – writer, wrinkled.
5) Rules: see above. There are few solid rules.

Links to writing
1), 2), 3) *Own answers*

5 Editing, proofreading
Comprehension
1) *Own answer*
2) Poet tree = poetry   strait = straight
   mist aches = mistakes   maid = made
   chequer = checker   nose = knows
   pea sea = pc   bee fore = before
   marques = marks   to = too
   four = for   putt = put
   revue = review   rite = right
   miss steaks = mistakes   rarely = really
   eye = i   threw = through
   sea = see   shore = sure
   quay = key   your = you're
   right = write   too = to
   weight = wait   no = know
   two = to   weigh = way
   weather = whether   tolled = told
   oar = or   sew = so
   write = right   sauce = source
3), 4), 5) *Own answers*

Language focus
1) Any ten from: chequer, pea sea, marques, four, revue, eye, sea, quay, right, wieght, two, weather, oar, write, straight, mist ache, maid, nose, bee fore, to, putt, rite, rarely, threw, shore, your, too, no, weigh, tolled, sew
2) a. Large tents set up for an outdoor gathering.
   b. A structure built on the bank of a waterway for use as a landing place.
   c. A golf stroke made on a putting green causing the ball to roll into the hole.
   d. A ceremonial act or action.
   e. To toll is to sound a bell by pulling a rope. (Multiple definitions possible)
3) a. eight
   b. saw/soar
   c. steal
   d. tale
   e. too/to
   f. their

g. air
h. practice
i. serial
j. stationery

4) **Homophones:** words that sound the same but have different spellings and meanings.
Homonyms: words that are spelled the same and pronounced the same but have different meanings.
Homographs: words that are spelled the same but have different meanings or pronunciations.

Links to writing
1), 2), 3), 4) *Own answers*

6 Point of view
Comprehension
1) The firefighters would see very little because they are behind their fire engine.
The journalist with the camera would see only the back of the red car.
The police officer would see more than the journalist with the camera, although his view is still mainly from behind the accident.
The character in the green shirt and blue trousers would see the front of the red car.
The driver of the lorry is higher up, so would see the front of the red car and all around him.
The driver of the red car would see the front of the lorry from very close up, but not much else.
The passenger in the back would see the back of the driver's head.
The girl, the boy on crutches, the girl holding his hand and the boy in the green shirt and orange trousers have the best view of the accident; they can see the lorry and the car from the side.
The man in blue coming from the helicopter would see the red car from behind.
2) Yes
3) The firefighters would only hear and, possibly, smell the accident.
The drivers and passenger would hear, see, feel and smell the accident.
All the other characters would see, hear and smell the accident.
4) None of the people at the accident will actually know the whole truth. Everybody would have a different viewpoint depending on where they are and how they are involved. E.g. while the driver of the lorry may have seen the whole event, he may be worried about being blamed and not tell the truth.
5) Each person will tell the story of the accident differently. Those directly involved in the accident (drivers, passenger) and those witnessing the accident taking place (bystanders) will use the first person. Those arriving on the scene after the accident (police officer, journalist) will use the third person so that their reports will seem more balanced.

Language focus
1), 2), 3), 4), 5) *Own answers*

Links to writing
1), 2) *Own answers*

7 Structures
Comprehension
1) The first paragraph describes the author's part of East London.
2) 'My part of East London has a character all its own' is the topic sentence and the rest of the paragraph develops the idea using details.
3) Paragraph two describes the railway arches. Paragraph three describes one particular railway arch.
4) The focus moves from East London then to the Docklands Light Railway, then the text focuses on the railway arches. The author finishes by describing one particular railway arch.
5) The text is a story because it is written in the present tense and describes a place rather than a person.

Language focus
1) *Own answer*
2) Speech is set out in paragraphs because it is easier to understand who says what. If speech is not in paragraphs the reader may get confused. Remember: new speaker, new line.

Links to writing
1), 2), 3) *Own answers*

8 Test your grammar, punctuation and spelling
Grammar

Use of the passive
1) The children organised the charity cake stall. A
2) The date was set. P
3) The cakes were provided by Mr Thomas. P
4) In total, £150 was donated to the chosen charity. P
5) The charity provides food for the homeless. A
6) The food parcels were delivered within a week. P
7) The parcels were appreciated. P
8) The children planned another event as it had been such a success. A

Punctuation

Using bullets to punctuate a list
Items to take with you:
• sunscreen
• swimming trunks or costume
• towel
• hat

Surfers need to have:
• a surfboard
• a wetsuit
• goggles
• a whistle.

What is the best sun protection?
• T-shirt
• wetsuit
• sunscreen
• sun umbrella

In the second list, a full stop has been added as the final item completes the sentence from the introductory stem.

Use of the semicolon
E.g. Tom liked going to the club; he particularly enjoyed the snooker matches.
Accept all correct and reasonable sentences.

Spelling

i before e
i before *e* except after *c* when the sound is /ee (but there are some exceptions).

1) deceive
2) receive
3) receipt
4) protein
5) ceiling
6) seize
7) deceit

protein and *seize* are exceptions.

Silent letters

	Examples Answers may include:	Rule
silent *k*	knee, knight	before *n*
silent *t*	listen, Christmas	after *s*
silent *g*	gnarled, gnome	before *n*
silent *b*	thumb, doubt	occurs after *m*, before *t*
silent *n*	autumn, hymn	after *m*
Another example of your choice	wreck, when, rhino, salmon, honest	

9 Formal and informal
Comprehension
1) Because there was a large log raft on it.
2) Generally: water comes out of a barrel; they have rafts; they have no modern conveniences; Huck does not appear to go to school.
3) He sold what he could find on the river.
4) He is violent and perhaps a drunk. He is nervous of strangers, which suggests he is in trouble of some sort.
5) Huck wants to be by himself, locked up in the hut so he can escape when his father goes.

6) The passage is conversational. Examples include: 'Well, I didn't see no way … '; 'I says to myself, I can fix it now … '.

Language focus
1) a. both of us being about wore out. 'Being' is incorrect. The past tense of 'to be' is 'were'. The past tense of the verb is 'worn out'.
b. if I could fix up some way to keep pap and the widow from trying to follow me. 'Fix up some way' is a colloquial expression.
c. it would be a certainer thing. The correct comparative is 'a more certain thing'.
d. Well, I didn't see no way for a while. The correct form is 'any way'. The original is a double negative.
e. That man warn't here for no good. I'd a shot him. The correct form is 'wasn't here for any good. I would have shot him'.
f. but what he had been saying give me the very idea. The correct past-tense form of the verb 'to give' here should be 'gave'.
2) a. but what he had been saying give me the very idea I wanted = gave me the very idea … (correct past tense of the verb)
b. I says to myself, I can fix it now = I said to myself … (correct past tense of the verb)
c. I can fix it now so nobody won't think of following me = so anybody won't think of … or so nobody will think of … (double negative in the original)
d. Anybody but pap would a waited = would have waited (a colloquialism)
e. but that warn't pap's style = wasn't pap's style (a colloquialism)
f. Nine logs was enough for one time = Nine logs were … (agreement of plural subject with verb)
g. then I out with my saw and went to work = got out my saw … (a colloquialism)
3) Huck Finn's story is best told in informal English. It is written in the first person and gives us a sense of his character as well as making it more real.

Links to writing
1), 2) *Own answers*

10 Devices to argue and persuade
Comprehension
1) People play competitive sport to win.
2) The author says it creates hatred, jealousy and boastfulness.
3) *Own answer*
4) He blames the spectators.
5) The author writes that spectators cheer their own side and boo the opposition.

Language focus
1) 'You play to win, and the game has little meaning unless you do your utmost to win'. Yes, speaking to the reader using **you** is more persuasive than using **I**.
2) 'Anyone who has played in a school football match knows this.' 'People want to see one side on top and the other side humiliated'.
3) These words signal to the reader that another argument is about to be made, focusing the reader's attention on the new argument.
4) '… are not the most savage combative instincts aroused?' Instead of presenting the argument, it brings the reader into the argument and makes them think about the issue personally.

Links to writing
1) *Own answer*

11 Cool reads
Comprehension
1) So you can find the book more easily if you want to read it.
2) Spy adventure book like a James Bond-type thriller.
3) It is action-packed, with mystery and humour. Generally exciting.
4) Alex is resourceful and likes gadgets. He is a teenager (14), his parents are dead and he lived with his uncle until he died too. He has become a spy.
5) Billionaire Herod Sayle is the villain. He is giving computers to every school but this is suspicious as we are not sure what he is trying to do.

6) They have multi-coloured noses because some have gone blue from the cold while others have gone red.
7) The author really means everything was covered with ice and was still.

Language focus
1) Simile: *'A dog trotted past like a ghost in a cloud'*
   Metaphor: *'Everything was rigid, locked-up and sealed'*
   Personification: *'low weak sun'*
2) **a.** A few minutes earlier
   b. When at last we reached
   c. Peering through the window
3) *Own answers*

Links to writing
1) *Own answer*

24 Words containing -ough
Comprehension
1) A kangaroo. It had a cough.
2) The correct spelling is **cough**, but **coff** has the same sound.
3) Because it sounds like Hoff in line 1. Rough
4) floo, Kangarough, armchere, tew, daid; *own answer for reason*
5) The messenger.
6) Words with the same pronunciation sometimes have different spellings.

Language focus
1) coff – cough; floo – flu; Kangarough – Kangaroo; armchere – armchair; tew – two; daid – dead; *own answer*
2) **a.** a zero – nought
   b. something not smooth – rough
   c. needed to make bread – dough
   d. to turn over soil – plough
   e. to be very careful – thorough
   f. an area in a town that governs itself – borough
   g. the process of thinking – thought
   h. in one side and out the other – through
3) Examples include:
   a. cough – scoff
   b. through – blue
   c. although – below
   d. bought – caught
   e. enough – stuff
   f. tough – fluff
4) *Own answer*

Links to writing
1), 2), 3) *Own answers*

25 Colons or semicolons
Comprehension
1) Pupils need to be clear that a colon is used to **introduce** something, e.g. a separate idea. It acts as a kind of pause. It can introduce a list of items or even some speech. A semicolon is part full stop and part comma. It **separates** main clauses and also breaks up long lists containing more than one word.
2) She could not reach the key on the table.
3) She needed a key to unlock the door and it was on the table. Unfortunately it was now out of her reach.
4) The table leg was slippery. It seemed that all hope was lost so she cried.
5) The cake said 'EAT ME', as if it had a life of its own. She did not know what would happen if she did eat it but either way it would have some kind of result.

Language focus
1) *'And its colours were strong: bold and harsh and sharply defined.'*
2) *Own answers*
3) **a.** The enemy was advancing: defeat was certain.
   b. He left really pleased with himself: everything was going well in his life.
4) *'Well, I'll eat it,' said Alice, 'and if it makes me grow larger, I can reach the key; and if it makes me grow smaller, I can creep under the door: so either way I'll get into the garden, and i don't care which happens!'*

Links to writing
1), 2) *Own answers*

26 Punctuation to clarify meaning – hyphen
Comprehension
1) If the punctuation is changed, the meaning of the sentences changes also.
2) When spoken, the sentences could all sound exactly the same.
3) Emphasis is important to make meaning clear. E.g. 'You will be required to work **twenty** four-hour shifts' means twenty shifts of four hours each. 'You will be required to work **twenty-four-hour** shifts' means that each shift will be 24 hours long.
4) Different punctuation can change the meaning of a sentence in unexpected and amusing ways. *'When I sing well, ladies feel sick'* means if he does a good job at singing then ladies will feel ill. *'When I sing, well ladies feel sick'* means no matter how he sings, healthy ladies in the audience will feel ill.

Language focus
1) **a.** The water tap is hot.
   The tap that gives hot water.
   b. Fifty $1 notes
   $50 notes
   c. The piano salesman is grand.
   The salesman sells grand pianos.
2) **a.** We order, merchandise and sell the products. (A list of three things they do.)
   We order merchandise, and sell the products. (Two things they do.)
   b. Have your car serviced today! Free oil included. (We encourage you to get your car serviced today, but oil is always included free in the service.)
   Have your car serviced! Today, free oil included. (Only today, you get free oil with your service.)
   c. I shall buy a car, in part-exchange for my wife. (He is purchasing a car by exchanging his wife for part of the value of the new vehicle.)
   I shall buy a car in part-exchange, for my wife. (He is purchasing a new car for his wife, by exchanging an old one.)
   d. 'The teachers,' said Emma 'should be quiet.' (Emma thinks the teachers should not make noise.) / The teachers said, 'Emma should be quiet'. (The teachers think Emma should not make noise.)
   e. We give quality service, and attention to detail. (The service is quality and they also pay attention to detail.)
   We give quality, service and attention to detail. (A list of three things they do.)

Links to writing
1) **a.** DANGER! NO SKATING ALLOWED.
   DANGER? NO. SKATING ALLOWED!
   b. 'Come and eat Barney,' said Mum.
   'Come and eat, Barney!' said Mum.
   c. 'Can you see Barney?' called Max through the fog.
   'Can you see, Barney?' called Max through the fog.
   d. Don't use commas, which are not necessary.
   Don't! Use commas which are not necessary.
2) *Own answer*

27 Revision: speech marks
Comprehension
1) A mother, father and their son, Chas, are in conversation. We are told that the father is speaking in the second paragraph and the mother's reaction to what he says is also given. Chas asks if he can go and see the old laundry.
2) The mother talks about the 'dive bomber' and the 'shelter' in the first paragraph.
3) Chas is keen to have a look at the crashed plane because his father's description makes the crash and explosion seem massive.
4) They let him go because he won't find anything but bricks; everything else has been destroyed.

5) 'gonner' instead of **dead**
   'cos' instead of **because**
   'me face' instead of **my face**
   'nowt' instead of **nothing**
   'D'you' instead of **Do you**
6) Non-standard English in speech is permitted because it recreates the natural or distinctive way in which people speak.

Language focus
1) By constantly saying who is speaking we lose the sense that this is natural speech. The writing becomes repetitive and slow. New speaker, new line makes it obvious who is speaking anyway.
2), 3) *Own answers*
4) If we are told how the characters look then we are able to understand how they feel and therefore how they are likely to speak. *Own answer*

Links to writing
1), 2) *Own answers*

28 Test your grammar, punctuation and spelling
Grammar
Question tags
1) You did say that you knew her, didn't you?
2) I think that's wrong, don't you? / isn't it?
3) He should get going, shouldn't he?
4) She can't be serious, can she?
5) I'm joining in, aren't I?
6) We're having fun, aren't we?

Punctuation
Hyphens to link words
co-owner
light-hearted, light-headed
seventy-eight
bad-tempered
quick-thinking, quick-tempered
muddle-headed
Own answers

Punctuation of speech (revision)
'Let's talk about monsters,' said Olly.
'Oh no, don't be an idiot. We'll just end up scaring ourselves to death!' yelled Cameron. At that point the lamps went out.
'Aaaagh!' screamed both boys.
'That's your fault, you idiot,' squeaked Cameron.
'No, it's our fault,' said voices from the distance. The boys looked at each other.
'Let's run!' they said together.

Spelling
Words ending in -ough
aw: bought, nought
uf: tough
off: cough
oo: through
u: thorough , borough
ow: plough, bough
oa: although, dough

Useful words
1) government
2) recommend
3) accommodate
4) correspond
5) marvellous
6) illustrate

4) The writer uses numbers to clearly identify the different stages of the experiment.
5) Some words are in brackets in the materials and procedure sections to give additional information, options or give a chemical's everyday name.

Language focus
1) *Own answer*
   The purpose of the text changes from inform to describe and the audience becomes somebody the writer knows rather than a stranger. Rewriting the instructions informally makes them more difficult to understand and follow because important information is lost in unnecessary details.
2) They use this type of writing because they want to make instructions as easy to understand as possible in case people have to read it quickly.
   a. A blow-up raft for babies is available if you need one.
   b. To keep safe, do what all the signs tell you to do.
   c. Press this button to get a crew member if you need help.
3) *Own answer*

Links to writing
1), 2), 3) *Own answers*

18 Biography: audience and purpose
1) You know that Hannah was Jewish because she attended Hebrew school and synagogue.
2) Hannah was gangly, tall, had creamy skin, brown hair and soft, brown eyes.
3) The central character in the biography is the main focus of the text, so it is important to know what they look like.
4) Her friend Anne was outspoken, impudent, and loved having fun.
5) Hannah was more interested in lessons while Anne was more interested in socialising and boyfriends.
6) Life was no longer simple for both of them because of the war and both of them being thirteen.
7) It was shocking that a law was passed so Jews were forbidden from working in most professions. It seems wrong that someone shouldn't be allowed to work because of their religion.

Language focus
1)

Feature	Evidence from text
Third person	*'She went to Hebrew school two times a week and to synagogue.'*
Personal details	*'She was gangly, tall, had creamy skin.'*
Past or present tense	*'Anne was outspoken …'*
Chronological structure	*'At age thirteen, This morning, Lately, no longer'*
Informal or formal language	*'Lately the differences between Hannah and Anne had become more pronounced.'*

2) *Own answer*

Links to writing
1) *Own answer*

19 Diaries: audience and purpose
Comprehension
1) Sarajevo is the capital of Bosnia and Herzegovina, which is located near the Adriatic Sea. After the break-up of Yugoslavia, many sides fought for power in the region.
2) A diary is set out by date, with events from the day discussed in the first person.
3) Zlata is talking to her diary.
4) She complains about being bored and the monotony of her life.
5) She dreams about her idol, Michael Jackson, and not being able to get his autograph. *Own answer*
6) Yes, the war seems very important to miss out of her diary.

Language focus
1)

Feature	Evidence from text
First person	*'I really do have to go to bed now!'*
Personal details	*'Everything is the same and keeps going in a circle (in my holiday life). Boredom, books, friends, phone calls and so on.'*
Past or present tense	*'We saw M&M and Needa off.'* *'I'm off to bed now.'*
Chronological order of events	*'Monday, 13 January 1992'* *'Tuesday, 14 January 1992'*
Formal or informal	*'Sad. Poor me. Ha, ha, ha …'*

2) Different tenses are used because the diary recounts things that happened in the past and also how the writer is feeling at the time of writing.

Links to writing
1), 2) *Own answers*

20 Ideas and supporting details
Comprehension
1) She was alone in the house because her father had gone to London.
2) It is important to know that her father was far away to emphasise how alone she was.
3) She looked in her wardrobe and under her bed to make sure that nobody or nothing was hiding.
4) This tells us that she is nervous about being alone.
5) The last line is a shock because we expect the room to be empty.
6) No, not identifying the voice makes it scarier.

Language focus
1) The writer uses these paragraphs because they are different topics.

Paragraph	Subject – what happens
1	We learn she is alone.
2	She secures her bedroom.
3	She dresses for bed.
4	She gets into bed, turns off the light.
5	A voice speaks.

The writer uses these paragraphs to mark clearly the different things that the girl does as she prepares to sleep.
2) *Own answer*
   Holding back important information until the end of the paragraph builds suspense.

Links to writing
1), 2) *Own answers*

21 Argument – using sentences to persuade
Comprehension
1) 120,000 people.
2) Over 400 chemicals, including tar, carbon monoxide and nicotine.
3) Lung cancer and heart disease.
4) Passive smoking is breathing in other people's cigarette smoke.
5) The writer wants a ban on smoking.
6) *Own answer*

Language focus
1) The passage becomes more like an information text that states facts, rather than a persuasive text.
2) Statement of fact: *'smoking causes 120,000 deaths in the UK each year.'*
   Using contrast: *'Surely you cannot deny the fact that smoking cigarettes increases the chance of suffering a heart attack by two to three times compared to a non-smoker?'*
   Using cause and effect: *'If we stopped it now, we would save 330 lives per day.'*
   Using conditional language: *'we should leave them to smoke if they want to.'*
   Using repetition: *'so I say it again: … passive smoking is dangerous.'*
   Using rhetorical questions: *'Surely you cannot deny the fact that smoking cigarettes increases the chance of suffering a heart attack by two*

to three times compared to a non-smoker?'
   Using personal language: *'you cannot deny'.*
3) *Own answer*

Links to writing
1) Statement of fact provides proof.
   Using contrast shows both sides of an argument.
   Using cause and effect demonstrates the consequences of a particular action.
   Using conditional language allows the writer to make opinions sound like facts.
   Using repetition emphasises a key point.
   Using a rhetorical question makes the answer to a question sound obvious.
   Personal language helps the writer form a closer relationship with the reader.
2) *Own answer*

22 Test your grammar, punctuation and spelling
Grammar
Cohesion across paragraphs
Tigers live in forests in India. They have been hunted almost to extinction in the wild, but increasing numbers are now living in protected areas or sanctuaries. Similarly, (G) elephants survive best in these types of areas.
On the other hand, (G) the African (S) terrain is trickier to use and monitor because it is so much larger than the Indian (S) jungles. As a consequence, (G) the World Wide Fund for Nature actively supports such (P) animals against hunters and being hunted and supports the development of protected areas.

Punctuation
Elision
1) fish and chips
2) 'I don't know … ,' replied the boy.
3) Did you ever see the film *That Will Be the Day*? It was amazing.
4) 'What are you looking at?' yelled the bully.
5) 'Hey, what do you mean?'
6) I love the song 'Shut Up Your Face!'

Using a dash rather than a comma
1) We all want to learn a sport – or so we say.
2) There was no other way – or was there?
3) Ashwyn, do you suppose you could – oh, never mind; I'll do it.
4) They sprinkled the powder everywhere and the ants disappeared – forever.
5) What he said was true – or so I thought.
6) They were all in agreement with the new plans – even agreeing to the shorter lunch breaks, but if anyone tried to change their holiday time, there would be trouble.

Spelling
Words ending in -fer
Answers may include:
1) referral, referring, reference, referee
2) preference, preferred, preferable, preferably
3) transference, transferable, transferral
4) deference, deferential

Homophones
1) advice
2) licence
3) practise
4) devices
5) illuminations
6) father

23 Using figurative language for impact
Comprehension
1) Winter
2) **Confections** mean 'any type of sweet foods'. The frost on the trees remind the author of sweets covered with sugar.
3) Sight: *'sparkling and motionless'*
   Smell: *'smelled like needles'*
   Hearing: *'solid sound'*
   Taste: *'confections of sugar'*
4) The dog reminded him of a ghost in a cloud because the dog's breath was warm and producing a cloud of vapour.
5) He describes the boys as *'wrapped like Russians'* to make us realise how cold it is and how many clothes they are wearing.

6) The book may be too violent or gory for some.

7) Full of action and suspense, this is a thrill-a-minute adventure.

Language focus

1), 2), 3), 4) *Own answers*

Links to writing

1), 2) *Own answers*

12 Writers from different times
Comprehension

1) The reader can recognise faces, clothing and the characters' names are used.

2) Romeo is the hero and Juliet is the heroine. The reader knows this because they are the main focus of the cartoon.

3) The cartoon shows how the characters interact, stand in relation to one another and their facial expressions.

4) No, the cartoon uses simplified English to aid understanding. There is less space in cartoons.

5) The names of the characters appear in bold and the reader is given a stage direction.

6) What the characters say to one another tells us how the characters should react to each other. E.g., Juliet says 'Come hither nurse', which tells us that the nurse is her servant.

7) It is not necessary to use playscript features in the cartoon because the reader can see the characters. Speech bubbles are used instead of characters' names in bold.

Language focus

1) a. Your mother wants to speak with you.
  b. Her mother is the most important woman in the house.
  c. Come here, nurse.
  d. Who's that man over there?

2) a. foolish or stupid
  b. a peasant
  c. deeply respectful
  d. abrasive
  e. poor or needy

Links to writing

1) *Own answer*

13 Writers from different places
Comprehension

1) The place they lived was remote and not many people lived there.

2) They knew '*there were many houses, candy and calico and other wonderful things*'.

3) Their father would trade furs in the store.

4) The snow and icicles tell you that it is winter.

5) Lighting the way and helping to milk the cow.

6) They were surprised because Sukey normally lived in the barn at that time of year.

Language focus

1), 2) *Own answers*

Links to writing

1) *Own answer*

14 Active and passive voice
Comprehension

1) Its purpose is to give a lot of accurate information in a few lines. It is about an experiment so should be impersonal.

2) You often find words such as *was, were, get, got* with the verbs.

3) Verbs are said to be in the 'active voice' because the subject of the sentence is actually performing the action. Verbs are said to be in the 'passive voice' because the thing or person that does the acting is not mentioned. Something **is being done** to the subject of the sentence.

4) In this kind of scientific writing, the most important thing is to explain what is happening in the experiment. Personal responses are not needed.

5) You may not know who is performing the action. You may not wish to mention it. It may be more polite.

Language focus

1) a. My rucksack is being inspected by the customs officer. The customs officer inspected my rucksack.

b. The store doors are guarded by two huge guards. Two huge guards guarded the store doors.

c. I was shown to my seat by a guide. The guide showed me to my seat.

d. In our class, children are helped by two assistants. Two assistants help children in our class.

e. The ancient Egyptian pot was dropped by the curator. The curator dropped the ancient Egyptian pot.

2) a. The vicar drove the car. The car was driven by the vicar.

b. New technology directs the police directly to the scene of the crime. The police are directed by new technology directly to the scene of the crime.

c. In the skyscraper, glass lifts take customers to the top. Customers are taken to the top of the skyscraper by glass lifts.

d. Our garages carry out all kinds of van repairs. All kinds of van repairs are carried out in our garages.

e. Thick fog delayed the departure of our plane. Our plane was delayed in departure by thick fog, or Our plane's departure was delayed by thick fog.

Links to writing

1), 2) *Own answers*

15 Test your grammar, punctuation and spelling
Grammar

Expanded noun phrases
Answers may include:
That extremely fierce sausage dog barked.
Some horrifically pink computer bags ripped.
Several very terrifying bloodhounds danced.
The very small sausage roll sneezed.

Punctuation
Ellipsis

	To show that a speaker didn't finish	To show a pause	To show words missed out
'I was just thinking … , ' murmured the girl.	✓		
The policeman said, '… he had been caught for a similar offence before.'			✓
Maya sat and watched … and watched … and watched.		✓	
'Hey … you … can you … hear … me?' yelled Ben.		✓	
The report said that in the great scheme of things … the expedition had gone well.			✓
'Turn to the right … no, to the left … no, the other way!' shouted Dan.		✓	

Colons
Example answer:
I have chosen four friends to come to my party: Olivia, Ellen, Katie and Elysia.
Accept all correct and reasonable sentences.

Spelling
Common words

1) special
2) financial
3) essential
4) vicious
5) delicious

Word families

Prefix	Examples of words	Origin and meaning of prefix
bi-	bicycle, biplane	Latin/two
tri-	tricycle, triangle	Latin, Greek/three
quad-	quadrant, quadruped	Latin/four
oct-	octagon, octopus	Greek/eight
cent-	centipede, centimetre	Latin/a hundred
uni-	unicycle, unit	Latin/one
milli-	millimetre, million	Latin/a thousand
dec-	decade, December	Latin/ten

16 Narrative techniques – third person
Comprehension

1) Drem knew the wolf was there because of the crashing of twigs and small branches.

2) The wolf swung its head from side to side, laid back its ears and had a wrinkled muzzle.

3) His foot came down on something sharp, stabbing through his shoe.

4) Drem didn't throw his spear because while he was regaining his balance the wolf sprang too close.

5) Drem's impression of the wolf was of '*a snarling head that seemed to fill his world – yellow fangs and a wet black throat.*'

6) The wolf injured him by hurting his right shoulder.

Language focus

1) No, the narrator is not a character in the story, which is being told in the third person. We are being given the narrator's point of view about the scene and Drem. The words that tell the reader this are it and him/his/he.

2) If you were being attacked by a wolf, you would not be able to describe all the details that are given here.

3) The narrator describes the gruesome appearance of the wolf and Drem's painful experience of stabbing his foot.

4) Quite what happened I never knew; it was all so quick, so hideously quick. My foot came down on something agonisingly sharp that stabbed through the soft raw-hide of my shoe and deep into my flesh – a torn furze root perhaps – throwing me for one instant off balance. It was only for the merest splinter of time, but twisting to regain my balance, somehow I missed my thrust; and the wolf was on me. I had one piercing flash of realisation; a vision of a snarling head that seemed to fill my world – yellow fangs and a wet black throat; and then sky and bushes spun over each other. I was half under the brute, I felt a searing, tearing pain in my right shoulder, I smelled death. The wolf's hot breath was on my face as I struggled wildly to shorten my spear for a dagger-stab, my chin jammed down in a despairing attempt to guard my throat; while at the same moment something in me – another Drem who was standing apart from all this – was knowing with a quiet and perfect clearness like a sky at summer evening: 'This is the end, then. It is Gault's fire for me …'
Realistically, a first-person narrator would not be able to give this much detail if they were being attacked in this way. The third person is more exciting here because the details help to build tension and paint a dramatic picture of the scene.

Links to writing

1) *Own answer*

17 Instructions: audience and purpose
Comprehension

1) A solute is a solid that dissolves in a liquid or solvent.

2) Baking soda.

3) The writing is set out in three sections, with each having a title. The first section gives background, the second tells the reader what materials they will need and the third section tells the reader how to do the experiment.

Colons

Write a beginning for each sentence, making sure that there is a complete sentence before the colon.

1) _____ : Olivia, Ellen, Katie and Elysia.

2) _____ : pizza, crisps, sausages and marshmallows.

3) _____ : Fridays, Saturdays and Sundays.

4) _____ : red, white and blue.

5) _____ : June, July and August.

6) _____ : snakes, frogs, toads and spiders.

Spelling

Common words

Choose and write out the correct spelling for each one. Think about how to spell /shul/ and /shus/.

Example

official   oficial   official

1) spetial   special   specal

2) finantial   financial   finansial

3) esential   essencal   essential

4) vicious   visious   vishus

5) delishious   delisious   delicious

Word families

Copy and complete the chart for these prefixes. An example is given.

Prefix	Examples of words	Origin and meaning of prefix
bi-	bicycle, biplane	Latin/two
tri-		
quad-		
oct-		
cent-		
uni-		
milli-		
dec-		

16 Narrative techniques – third person

From *Warrior Scarlet*

This book is set in the Bronze Age – several thousand years ago. Drem is a boy whose arm is crippled. Here he is on a wolf hunt.

And suddenly the wolf was there. With a crashing of twigs and small branches it sprang into the open, then, seeing the hunters all about it, checked almost in mid-spring, swinging its head from side to side, with laid-back ears and wrinkled muzzle: a great, brindled dog wolf, menace in every raised hackle. Then, as though it knew with which of the hunters it had to deal, as though it expected him, it looked full at Drem. For a long moment it stood there, tensed to spring, savage amber eyes on his as though it knew and greeted him. The rest of the band had checked at a small distance, spears ready; but Drem was no longer aware of them; only of the wolf, his wolf.

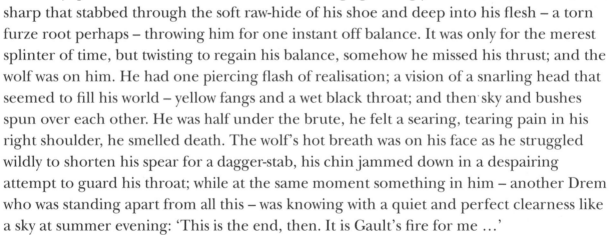

…

It seemed to him that the open jaws with their lolling tongue were grinning at him as he leapt forward and ran in low, his spear drawn back to strike. And at the same instant the wolf sprang.

Quite what happened he never knew; it was all so quick, so hideously quick. His foot came down on something agonisingly sharp that stabbed through the soft raw-hide of his shoe and deep into his flesh – a torn furze root perhaps – throwing him for one instant off balance. It was only for the merest splinter of time, but twisting to regain his balance, somehow he missed his thrust; and the wolf was on him. He had one piercing flash of realisation; a vision of a snarling head that seemed to fill his world – yellow fangs and a wet black throat; and then sky and bushes spun over each other. He was half under the brute, he felt a searing, tearing pain in his right shoulder, he smelled death. The wolf's hot breath was on his face as he struggled wildly to shorten his spear for a dagger-stab, his chin jammed down in a despairing attempt to guard his throat; while at the same moment something in him – another Drem who was standing apart from all this – was knowing with a quiet and perfect clearness like a sky at summer evening: 'This is the end, then. It is Gault's fire for me …'

Rosemary Sutcliff

Speak about it

Who is telling the story? How do you know?

Who is the story about?

Are they the same person?

Does the character have a name or not?

How is this way of telling a story different from a first-person narrator, e.g. someone who starts a story, 'I … '?

Does having a narrator like this make the story different? Give some reasons.

Comprehension

1) How did Drem know that the wolf was there?

2) What kind of things did the wolf do when it knew that it was trapped?

3) What happened to make Drem fall?

4) Why didn't Drem throw his spear?

5) What was Drem's impression of the wolf when it attacked him?

6) How did the wolf injure Drem?

Language focus

1) Is the narrator a character in the story? Whose point of view are we being given in the story? Identify the words that tell us.

2) A third-person narrator can explain what is going on around the character in a lot more detail than a first-person narrator. Find examples of this in the third paragraph. For example, if you were being attacked by a wolf, how much of this would you be able to describe at the moment?

3) Third-person narrators are often better for explaining the internal thoughts and feelings of a character in a tense situation. Find examples of how the description appeals to our senses in the passage, so we get a sense of how the character feels.

4) Why is this level of explanation difficult if you are using the first person I form? Rewrite the third paragraph using the first person, the I form. What difference does this make, if any, to the excitement of the description?

Links to writing

1) Plan the rest of the story. Use a diagram to help. What other questions would you need to answer in your planning?

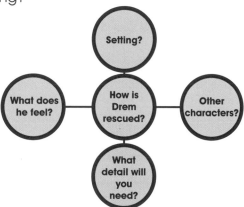

17 Instructions: audience and purpose

To grow crystals from a supersaturated solution

A solid that dissolves in a liquid or **solvent** is called a **solute**.

Materials

2 tall narrow jars

tweezers

kettle

rubber band

pencil

spoon

thread

washer or paperclip
(optional)

coffee filter papers

magnifying glass

sugar

sodium chloride
(salt)

magnesium
sulphate
(Epsom salts)

sodium bicarbonate
(baking soda)

Procedure

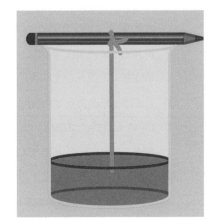

This experiment will take a few days to complete. If you are having difficulty forming crystals, try tying a small washer or paperclip to the end of the string.

1 Fill one jar with hot water and stir in one of the salts until no more salt will dissolve.

2 Tie one end of the thread to the middle of a pencil and carefully hang the thread in the solution so it is not touching the bottom or the sides.

3 When no more crystals have grown on the thread, remove and place it on a coffee filter paper.

4 Pour the liquid into a second jar, being careful not to pour out any crystals.

5 Carefully scrape the crystals off the thread (or remove any off the bottom of the jar) and examine them using a magnifying glass.

6 If large-enough single crystals are formed, tie one to some thread and hang it in the saved saturated solution to see if it grows over the following days.

Speak about it

What is the purpose of this piece of writing?
Who is it aimed at?
Would you describe the writing as formal or informal? Explain why.

Comprehension

1) What is a solute?

2) What is another name for sodium bicarbonate?

3) How is the writing set out to make reading and understanding easier?

4) Why does the writer use numbers in explaining the procedure?

5) Why are some words in brackets in the materials section and in the procedure section?

Language focus

1) Rewrite part of the experiment informally, e.g. 'We took some absolutely boiling water, put in lovely white salt and gave it a stir.' What differences to the purpose and audience would this make? Why is this not appropriate to a science experiment?

2) Here are some examples of formal language found on a plane. Why do they use such language? Write the expressions in everyday language.
   a. Infant flotation devices available.
   b. For your safety you must comply with all signs.
   c. Press button to summon crew member if assistance is required.

3) Write two descriptions: a tree trunk and a flower. The first description is for a science lesson and the second will appear in a story. How will they be different? Consider your audience.

Links to writing

1) Write a set of instructions in formal English that you would find in a box when you buy a new product, e.g. how to play a DVD.

2) Write the same instructions in a letter to a friend, starting: 'I bought a new DVD player the other day. It was dead easy to use. All you do is …'

3) Use a computer to produce both types of writing described in questions 1 and 2 as they would normally be seen. Display them side by side and highlight:

the differences in formal and informal language

the suitability for the purpose of the writing

the suitability for each different audience.

18 Biography: audience and purpose

From *Hannah Goslar Remembers*

At age thirteen Hannah Goslar was fun-loving but also quite religious. She went to Hebrew school two times a week and to synagogue. She was gangly, tall, had creamy skin, and brushed her mahogany brown hair so fast that electric sparks crackled. Hannah's best features were her soft, brown eyes.

This morning she was going to call for her friend, Anne Frank. Anne was outspoken, even impudent; she loved having fun. She was more interested in socialising and boyfriends than Hebrew lessons. Lately the differences between Hannah and Anne had become more pronounced. With the war raging and both of them being thirteen, life was not as simple as it used to be when they were little girls sitting side by side in school.

Hannah had kissed her father before she left the house. Because of a new law that Jews were forbidden from working in most professions, Mr Goslar was no longer allowed to work as a professional economist. This meant that it was difficult for him to support his family.

Alison Leslie Gold

Speak about it

Who is this passage about?
Who is the narrator? Is it the same person?
What is the purpose of this kind of writing?
What kind of information does it give?
Is the historical background important?
Which tense is it written in?
Would you say this text is formal or informal in its style?
Why do you think people write biographies of some people but not of others?
Find examples of biographies in the library to see if you can reach a conclusion.

Comprehension

1) How do you know what religion Hannah followed?

2) What did Hannah look like?

3) Why is it important to be able to imagine what characters look like in biographies?

4) What was Hannah's friend Anne like?

5) What were some of the differences between Hannah and Anne?

6) Why was life no longer so simple for Hannah and Anne?

7) Do you find anything shocking in the third paragraph? Explain carefully.

Language focus

1) Complete a chart with evidence to show some features of biography.

Feature	Evidence from text
Third person	
Personal details	
Past or present tense	
Chronological structure	
Informal or formal language	

2) Find out more about Anne Frank. You could use the Internet or read her diary. How will you decide which are the most important pieces of information to use? Plan and write the first chapter of a biography of Anne Frank using the features discussed and identified in your work here.

Links to writing

1) Research and write the biography of someone you admire.

   Use books and the Internet to research them.

   Write notes and then sort them into the facts you will use. A flow chart may help.

   How will you structure the biography?

   Will you start at the beginning of the person's life and move in chronological order?

   Will you start at the person's death and move backwards?

19 Diaries: audience and purpose

From *Zlata's Diary: A Child's Life in Sarajevo*

Zlata lived in Sarajevo in the early 1990s when there was a war.

Diary

Monday, 13 January 1992

We saw M&M and Needa off. AUHHHH! It's been a long day! I'm off to bed now – it's 23.10. I'm reading *Captain at Fifteen* by Jules Verne.

Everything is the same and keeps going in a circle (in my holiday life). Boredom, books, friends, phone calls and so on. I really do have to go to bed now! GOOD NIGHT AND SWEET DREAMS!

Tuesday, 14 January 1992

I yawned, opened my pen and started to write: I'm listening to music from Top Gun on 'Good Vibrations' [on the radio]. Something else is on now. I've just destroyed the back page of *Bazar* [a fashion magazine]. I talked to Mummy on the phone. She's at work.

I have something to tell you. Every night I dream that I'm asking Michael Jackson for his autograph, but either he won't give it to me or his secretary writes it, and then all the letters melt, because Michael Jackson didn't write them. Sad. Poor me. Ha, ha, ha …

Zlata Filipovic

Speak about it

Who is this passage about?
Who is the narrator? Is it the same person?
What is the purpose of this kind of writing?
What kind of information does it give?
Is the historical background important?
Which tense is it written in?
Would you say this was formal or informal in its style? Why?

Comprehension

1) Where is Sarajevo and why was there a war there? Look in an atlas or on the Internet to find out.

2) How is a diary set out?

3) Who is Zlata 'talking' to in her diary?

4) What does Zlata complain about? Do you complain about the same things?

5) What does Zlata dream about? Do you dream about the same kind of things?

6) Does it surprise you that Zlata does not write about the war? Why?

Language focus

1) Complete a chart with evidence to show the features of a diary.

Feature	Evidence from text
First person	
Personal details	
Past or present tense	
Chronological order of events	
Formal or informal language	

2) Why are different tenses used in the diary?

Links to writing

1) After reading a book, pick a character that you would like to be. Write down a list of their characteristics, especially paying close attention to how the character talks or writes.

2) Imagine that you are a sportsperson or a pop star. Write your diary for a week.

What did you do?

What was the weather like?

Who else was with you?

Did anything exciting happen?

How did you feel?

20 Ideas and supporting details

From *Boo!*

She didn't like it at all when her father had to go down to London and, for the first time, she had to sleep alone in the old house.

She went up to her bedroom early. She turned the key and locked the door. She latched the windows and drew the curtains. She peered inside her wardrobe, and pulled open the bottom drawer of her chest-of-drawers; she got down on her knees and looked under the bed.

She undressed; she put on her nightdress.

She pulled back the heavy linen cover and climbed into bed. Not to read but to try and sleep – she wanted to sleep as soon as she could. She reached out and turned off the lamp.

'That's good,' said a little voice. 'Now we're safely locked in for the night.'

Kevin Crossley-Holland

Speak about it

What is the story about?
Is it a complete story? Can you identify the story structure, e.g. **a beginning, middle, climax, resolution**?
Would it be possible to write it in an even shorter version?
How many paragraphs are there?
What is the subject of each one? Is each paragraph different?
Why do we divide written work into paragraphs?

Comprehension

1) Why was she alone in the house?

2) Why is it important to know that her father was a long way away?

3) Why did she look in her wardrobe and under her bed?

4) What does this tell us about how she felt about being alone?

5) Why is the last line a shock?

6) Does it matter that 'the little voice' is not identified?

Language focus

1) This writer has deliberately written a very short story to create a mystery. Make a chart showing what happens in each paragraph.

Paragraph	Subject – what happens
1	
2	
3	
4	
5	

How does this help you to see why the writer has used the paragraphs he has?

2) Change the beginnings of each paragraph by altering the sentence structure, e.g. 'When her father had to …' What difference does this make? Does it make the passage any less scary?

Links to writing

1) Copy Kevin Crossley-Holland's model and write your own very short story in five paragraphs.

2) Write three more paragraphs.

A new character arrives.

Two characters speak.

A new event occurs.

21 Argument – using sentences to persuade

BAN SMOKING! IT KILLS!

It is an indisputable fact that smoking causes 120,000 deaths in the UK each year. If we stopped it now, we would save 330 lives per day.

Many well-informed people know that smoking causes more than 40 types of illnesses and has around 20 ways of killing you because cigarettes contain over 400 chemicals, including tar, carbon monoxide (includes cyanide and arsenic) and nicotine. *Therefore*, 30% of all cancer deaths are related to smoking.

Surely you cannot deny the fact that smoking cigarettes increases the chance of suffering a heart attack by two to three times compared to a non-smoker?

Objectors might say that people have a right to decide their own health and we should leave them to smoke if they want to. *But this would be to ignore* the very real dangers of passive smoking, which causes several hundred cases of lung cancer and several cases of heart disease in non-smokers in the UK each year. I believe that low-tar cigarettes pose an equal threat – so I say it again: … passive smoking is dangerous. Countries that have banned smoking see a huge health gain.

In conclusion, around half of all cigarette smokers will eventually be killed by the habit – as well as other innocent people around them if we do not ban smoking immediately.

Writer is introducing their view.

This might be true – it is written to seem like a fact to add weight to the argument.

Gives a reason – cause and effect. The use of detail adds weight to the argument.

Rhetorical question – does not need an answer – makes it sound obvious.

Writer concludes their argument. (Is it the right one?)

Strong title that gives the point of view.

This is a fact that can be proved. Gives the impression that the argument is correct.

Writer is giving his own view in such a way as to encourage acceptance.

Concludes that stage of the point of view.

Writer introduces a possible argument against his view. But counters it.

Opinion given as fact.

Speak about it

What is the purpose of this piece of writing? What does it aim to do?

How much information does it contain? Which facts grab your attention?

Does the writer use fact or opinion or a mixture of both? For what purpose does the writer use this approach?

Which words make the argument particularly persuasive?

Do the paragraphs in this particular order help strengthen the argument?

Comprehension

1) How many people die each year from smoking in the UK?

2) What is in cigarettes that can cause you to become ill?

3) What kinds of diseases can they cause?

4) What is **passive smoking**?

5) What does the writer want doing about the problem?

6) Does the writer's argument convince you? If so, why?

Language focus

1) Take away the words in italics. Is the passage still an argument? Is it persuasive in any way?

2) Find examples of the following in the passage: using statements of fact, using contrast, using cause and effect, using conditional language (e.g. **If … then**), using repetition, using rhetorical questions, using personal language in the second person (**you**).

3) Using the same features of style, write a passage that argues that children should not be forced to wear school uniform.

   Decide what will be in each paragraph.

   Think of arguments both for and against.

   Find evidence to back up your arguments.

   Start each paragraph in a different persuasive way.

   Use connectives that help develop your argument, e.g. therefore, however, moreover.

Links to writing

1) Explain how each of the features of style in question 2 above helps to create a persuasive argument.

2) Plan a persuasive text to encourage others in your school to support an environmental organisation or event that you think is worthwhile. You may need to do some research on the Internet.

   List the main points you want to make.

   Collect information to support each point.

   Make notes about your audience.

   Present your persuasive text in the form of a leaflet.

   Publish it using a computer.

   Include all the features you have discussed in this passage.

22 Test your grammar, punctuation and spelling

Cohesion across paragraphs

Which kinds of cohesion can you find in the text? Copy it out and write G, S or P above each example.

> **G** for grammatical cohesion, e.g. using an adverbial to link ideas in, or between, paragraphs.
>
> **S** for semantic cohesion, e.g. using repetition of a word or phrase to link ideas in, or between, paragraphs.
>
> **P** for pronouns, e.g. to refer back to noun phrases in a previous paragraph.

Tigers live in forests in India. They have been hunted almost to extinction in the wild, but increasing numbers are now living in protected areas or sanctuaries. Similarly, elephants survive best in these types of areas. On the other hand, the African terrain is trickier to use and monitor because it is so much larger than the Indian jungles. As a consequence, the World Wide Fund for Nature actively supports such animals against hunters and being hunted and supports the development of protected areas.

Punctuation

Elision: informal and formal language

Write out the full versions of these sentences or phrases that use elision.

1) fish 'n' chips

2) 'I dunno ... ,' replied the boy.

3) Did you ever see the film *That'll Be the Day?* It was amazin'.

4) 'Whatyer lookin' at?' yelled the bully.

5) 'Hey, whachyermean?'

6) I love the song 'Shaddap You Face!'

Using a dash rather than a comma

A dash is longer than a hyphen. Write each sentence, adding a dash.

1) We all want to learn a sport or so we say.

2) There was no other way or was there?

3) Ashwyn, do you suppose you could oh, never mind; I'll do it.

4) They sprinkled the powder everywhere and the ants disappeared forever.

5) What he said was true or so I thought.

6) They were all in agreement with the new plans even agreeing to the shorter lunch breaks, but if anyone tried to change their holiday time, there would be trouble.

Spelling

Words ending in -fer

Write each word with two different endings.

1) refer

2) prefer

3) transfer

4) defer

Homophones

Choose the right homophone to complete the sentence and write it.

1) He gave the best **(advise/advice)** he knew.

2) Don't forget that you need to buy a TV **(license/licence)**.

3) If you want to play the piano really well, you must **(practise/practice)** every day.

4) I love reading about all the technology **(devices/devises)** being developed.

5) Switch on the **(illuminations/eliminations)**!

6) He's my **(farther/father)**.

23 Using figurative language for impact

This writer uses figurative language – figures of speech **such as similes and metaphors. These are both kinds of comparisons. Similes use** like **or** as **to compare. Metaphors make a more positive statement. Look at the examples in the passage.**

From *Cider with Rosie*

It was a world of glass, sparkling and motionless. Vapours had frozen all over the trees and transformed them into confections of sugar. Everything was rigid, locked-up and sealed, and when we breathed the air it **smelled like**

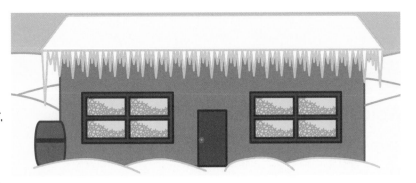

needles and **stabbed our nostrils** and made us sneeze.

Having sucked a few icicles, and kicked the water-butt – to hear its solid sound – and breathed through the frost on the window-pane, we ran up into the road. We hung around, waiting for something to happen. A dog trotted past like a ghost in a cloud, panting his aura around him. The distant fields in the low weak sun were crumpled like oyster shells.

Presently some more boys came to join us, wrapped like Russians, with multi-coloured noses. We stood round in a group and just gasped at each other, waiting to get an idea. The thin ones were blue, with hunched up shoulders, hands deep in their pockets, shivering. The fat ones were rosy and blowing like whales; all of us had wet eyes. What should we do? We didn't know.

Laurie Lee

Speak about it

What is the passage describing?
Why doesn't the writer just state the facts?
How many different ways does the writer begin sentences?
Find examples of short sentences. Why does the writer use them?
Find examples of longer sentences. Why does the writer choose to make them longer?
How many comparisons, e.g. **similes**, can you find?

Comprehension

1) What season is the author describing?

2) What does **confections** mean? What kind of thing did the frost on the trees remind the author of?

3) What senses is the author using in his description? Give some examples.

4) What did the dog remind the author of? Why?

5) Why does the author describe the boys as 'wrapped like Russians'?

6) Why do the boys have 'multi-coloured noses'?

7) What does the author really mean by 'It was a world of glass'?

Language focus

1) Find examples in the passage of where the writer uses other similes, metaphors or personification (where something is given human characteristics) to develop sentences and make them more interesting.

2) Adverbial phrases normally, but not always, occur at the beginning of a paragraph. Identify the adverbial phrases in the following.
   a. A few minutes earlier, the car had been sparkling clean.
   b. When at last we reached the safety of the cave, we dropped down in the sand.
   c. Peering through the window, the prisoner saw the hangman coming to collect him.

3) Use the following as sentence openers.
   a. Slipping in the snow,   c. After a while,
   b. Chomping on an apple,   d. Without any warning,

Links to writing

1) Write a highly descriptive passage about what you and your friends did in a summer scene, e.g. **at the beach**, **playing by the side of a river**.

   Paragraph 1: Use a bold opening statement using metaphor. Include descriptive sentences about the scene and what it reminded you of, using more than one sense.

   Paragraph 2: Describe some actions, what you did, what you saw and heard, what things reminded you of …

   Paragraph 3: Some other people join you. What happens? What do they look like or remind you of?

24 Words containing -ough

There can be problems in spelling because some phonemes can be spelled in more than one way, and the same spelling can be used for more than one phoneme. Let's investigate a silly example!

A Poem for Children Ill in Bed

The eminent Professor Hoff
Kept, as a pet, a Kangaroo
Who, one March day, started a coff
That very soon turned into floo.

Before the flu carried him off
To hospital (still with his coff)
A messenger came panting through
The door and saw the Kangarough.

The Kangaroo lay wanly there
Within the Prof's best armchere
Taking (without the power to chew)
A sip of lemonade or tew.

'O Kangaroo,' the fellow said
'I'm glad you're not already daid,
For I have here (pray do not scoff)
Some stuff for your infernal coff.'

Anthony Thwaite

Speak about it

What is a **phoneme**?
What is a **letter string**?
What examples can you find in the poem of phonemes being spelled in more than one way?
Why can this cause problems with spelling?
Do you have any ways of remembering how to spell such words?

Comprehension

1) What did the professor keep as a pet? What was wrong with his pet?

2) What do you notice about the spelling of the word to describe this? How do you spell it correctly?

3) Why do you think the poet thought it might be spelled in this way? What other word is spelled like these two words and makes the same sound?

4) List other words used in the poem that you think might not be spelled correctly. Why do you think the author wrote them in this way?

5) Who came to solve the pet's problem?

6) What point is the poet trying to make in his poem?

Objective focus

1) List the words in the poem that are not spelled correctly. Write the correct versions. What do you think happens to your reaction to the poem now?

2) Find words that match the meanings below. Check the spelling of your answers.

   a. a zero **b.** something not smooth **c.** needed to make bread **d.** to turn over soil
   e. to be very careful **f.** an area in a town that governs itself **g.** the process of thinking
   h. in one side and out the other

3) Find words that rhyme, not using the same letter string, with these.

   a. cough   **b.** through   **c.** although   **d.** bought   **e.** enough   **f.** tough

4) Find more examples using the **-ough** phoneme, where the words sound different.

Links to writing

1) These words have common letter strings but each can be pronounced differently. Use a dictionary to write sentences to show the two meanings for each word.

   a. lead   **b.** wind   **c.** row   **d.** sow   **e.** bow

2) Try writing a few more verses for the poem.

   Work out the poem's pattern, e.g. number of lines, rhyme scheme and rhythm.

3) Write sentences using these words to show that you know what they mean.

   a. rough   **b.** borough   **c.** ought   **d.** nought   **e.** though   **f.** plough

25 Colons or semicolons

Adapted from *Alice's Adventures in Wonderland*

Alice finds herself in Wonderland but she has shrunk!

After a while, finding that nothing more happened, she decided on going into the garden at once; but, alas for poor Alice! When she got to the door, she found she had forgotten the little golden key, and when she went back to the table for it, she found she could not possibly reach it: she could see it quite plainly through the glass, and she tried her best to climb up one of the legs of the table, but it was too slippery; and when she had tired herself out with trying, the poor little thing sat down and cried.

Soon her eye fell on a little glass box that was lying under the table: she opened it, and found in it a very small cake, on which the words 'EAT ME' were beautifully marked in currants. 'Well, I'll eat it,' said Alice, 'and if it makes me grow larger, I can reach the key; and if it makes me grow smaller, I can creep under the door: so either way I'll get into the garden, and I don't care which happens!'

Lewis Carroll

Speak about it

From which two punctuation marks is a semicolon made? How is a semicolon different from a comma or a full stop?
From which two punctuation marks is a colon made? How is a colon different from a comma or a full stop?
Why not use a comma or a full stop? What extra do semicolons or colons add to the meaning or effect of a passage?
Can you identify any rules for the use of semicolons and colons?

Comprehension

1) Identify all the semicolons and colons in the passage. Would you have used other punctuation? Why?

2) Find some evidence in the passage to prove that Alice has shrunk.

3) Why couldn't Alice get to the garden? What did she need? Where was it?

4) Why could she not climb the table? How did she feel about this? Find evidence.

5) What was strange about what was written on the cake? What did Alice think it would do if she ate it?

Language focus

1) Colons introduce a list of items or can give you more information about what has just been said. Find examples in the passage to prove this definition.

2) Complete these sentences after the colon with suitable information.
   a. The jungle was amazing: …
   b. This was what was underneath her bed: …

3) Sometimes colons are used when one clause explains another. Rewrite these two examples using a colon.
   a. The enemy was advancing. Defeat was certain.
   b. He felt really pleased with himself. Everything was going well in his life.

4) Semicolons are used instead of full stops to separate two closely linked main clauses of similar importance, or to break up long and complicated items in a list. Find an example in the passage to prove this definition.

Links to writing

1) Continue Alice's story. What happens when she eats the cake? Does it make her grow or shrink? What are the results of this? Use colons to introduce new ideas and expand upon the detail.

2) Alice meets some strange creatures in Wonderland. Imagine that she is chased by a large cat when she is very small. Describe the exciting chase. Use long sentences to build tension, but divide them using semicolons. Ask a friend to check your work and comment on whether you have been successful.

26 Punctuation to clarify meaning – hyphen

Read the examples carefully.

What difference does the punctuation make to the meaning?

Look carefully at the examples. What are the differences in punctuation between each one?

How does the different punctuation change the meaning in each case?

What is the effect of this?

What would happen to the meaning if you took away all the punctuation?

Comprehension

1) How do these examples show that it is important to use punctuation carefully?

2) How could some of the examples be very confusing if you were just speaking them?

3) How could you emphasise the correct punctuation if you were speaking these statements?

4) Why does it make some of these statements amusing? Give reasons.

Language focus

1) Show how these words can be presented in two different ways to create different meanings. Look at the examples on the opposite page to see how hyphens can help.

   a. hot water tap

   b. fifty dollar notes

   c. grand piano salesman

2) Rewrite these sentences using different punctuation to give at least two different meanings. Explain how each is different.

   a. We order merchandise and sell the products.

   b. Have your car serviced today free. Oil included.

   c. I shall buy a car in part-exchange for my wife.

   d. The teachers said Emma should be quiet.

   e. We give quality service and attention to detail.

Links to writing

1) Punctuate these in two ways to mean two very different things.

   a. **DANGER**

   NO

   SKATING ALLOWED

   b. Come and eat Barney said Mum.

   c. Can you see Barney called Max through the fog?

   d. Don't use commas which are not necessary.

2) Write a story in which confusion over punctuation leads to a very embarrassing situation. You could use one of the examples above.

27 Revision: speech marks

From *The Machine Gunners*

This story takes place in the Second World War. Chas listens to his parents talk about a bombing.

'I thought we were a gonner last night, I really did. That dive bomber … I thought it was going to land on top of the shelter … Mrs Spalding had one of her turns.'

'It wasn't a dive bomber,' announced Father with authority. 'It had two engines. He came down on the rooftops 'cos one of the RAF lads was after him. Right on his tail. You could see his guns firing. And he got him. Crashed on the old laundry at Chirton. Full bomb load. I felt the heat on me face a mile away.' Mother's face froze.

'Nobody killed, love. That laundry's been empty for years. Just as well – there's not much left of it.'

Chas finished his last carefully-cut slice of fried bread and looked hopefully at his father.

'Can I go and see it?'

'Aye, you can go and look. But you won't find nowt but bricks. Everything just went.'

Mother looked doubtful. 'D'you think he should?'

'Let him go, lass. There's nowt left.'

'No unexploded bombs?'

'No, a quiet night really. Lots of our fighters up. That's why you didn't hear any guns.'

Robert Westall

Speak about it

What special punctuation marks do you need to punctuate speech?
Why do you think this is necessary?
How should speech be set out when you are writing it?
How do you know who is speaking in the passage, even if their names are not written down?
Which words tell you how the characters might have spoken the words?
Do any words tell you how the characters may have felt?

Comprehension

1) Who are the people speaking in this passage? What tells you this?

2) What evidence is there to show that this story is set in the Second World War?

3) Why do you think Chas is so keen to have a look at the crashed plane?

4) Why do his parents let him go in the end?

5) What slang words can you find in the passage?

6) Why is it permitted to use non-standard English in speech but not in other kinds of writing?

Language focus

1) Rewrite the last section of the dialogue, but write who said the words, e.g. **said Mother**, **replied Father**. How does this make a difference in the speech? Does it slow it down? Does it make it seem too obvious?

2) Write a piece of dialogue between two friends that only uses their words in speech marks and does not comment on them or how they said the words, e.g. no **said Alex**, **replied Tracy**. What information do you have to include in the speech to make sure the reader gets the correct impression?

3) Rewrite the speech from question 2 using Standard English. How does this make a difference? How much of a sense of the characters or the place do you lose?

4) Chas 'looked hopefully'. His mother 'looked doubtful'. How do these clues help us to read the tone of the speech and understand how the characters were feeling? Choose some different words to include. Does the speech have to be changed to make their new feelings clear?

Links to writing

1) Continue the dialogue in the scene, following the same style and the same use of language.
   Make sure that Chas' mum expresses some more concerns about him going.
   Chas has to defend himself and his father supports him.
   What warnings would his parents give him?

2) Write a new scene of dialogue using some of the things you have discussed from the extract. In the book, Chas finds the German who was piloting the crashed plane.

28 Test your grammar, punctuation and spelling

Grammar

Question tags

Add question tags to these sentences. Write them out to make them more informal and with correct punctuation.

Example

| **I really don't know what to say about that.** | → | **I really don't know what to say about that, *do you?*** |

1) You did say that you knew her.

2) I think that's wrong.

3) He should get going. .

4) She can't be serious.

5) I'm joining in.

6) We're having fun.

Punctuation

Hyphens to link words

Form six words from the following.

| bad | muddle | owner | eight | light | quick |
| hearted | thinking | headed | seventy | co | tempered |

Example   **bad-tempered**

Write a sentence for each of these new words.

Punctuation of speech

Spot the errors and write the sentences out correctly.

> Lets talk about monsters said Olly. Oh no, don't be an idiot, we'll just end up scaring ourselves to death yelled Cameron. At that point the lamps went out. Aaaagh screamed both boys. That's your fault you idiot squeaked Cameron. No, it's our fault said voices from the distance. The boys looked at each other. Let's run they said together.

Spelling

Words ending in -ough

There are different ways to pronounce **-ough** in words. Sort these words and write each into the correct group: **aw   uf   off   oo   u   ow   oa**

plough   cough   through   thorough   tough   bought   nought   although borough   bough   dough

Useful words

Choose and write out the correct spelling for each one.

Example

| parliament | parlement | parliment |

1) goverment	government	guvernment
2) recomend	recommend	reccomend
3) accommodate	acommodate	accomodate
4) corespond	coresppond	correspond
5) marvelous	marvallous	marvellous
6) committee	comitee	commitee

Glossary

active voice   when it's clear who or what the verb relates to in a sentence or phrase (subject, verb, object)

ambiguity   when meaning is unclear because it can be interpreted in more than one way

antonym   a word or phrase that means the opposite of another word or phrase in the same language

bracket   a punctuation mark that is used in pairs to separate or add information (like this)

bullet point   a punctuation mark usually used to make key information clear in a list

cohesion   joining information together

cohesive device   a word used to show how the different parts of a text fit together

colon   mainly used between two main clauses in cases where the second clause explains or follows from the first; to introduce a list; before a quotation, and sometimes before direct speech. See Punctuation chart

dash   a punctuation mark that is used – often informally – to add a comment or information in writing. See Punctuation chart

determiner   a determiner modifies a noun, e.g. **the**, **a**, **an**, **this**, **those**, **my**, **your**, **some**, **every** or numerals

etymology   a word's history and origin

hyphen   used to link words and parts of words, and mainly used in compound words to join prefixes to other words or to show word breaks

modal verb   a modal verb changes the meaning of other verbs as it tells us about how certain, able or obliged something or someone is, e.g. **will**, **would**, **can**, **could**, **may**, **might**, **shall**, **should**, **must** and **ought**

morphology   considering how a word is made up of different parts

object   the person or thing affected by the verb

parenthesis   an extra word, clause or sentence inserted into a passage to give non-essential information

passive voice   a passive verb is the opposite of active – it has a subject that is undergoing the action of the verb, rather than carrying it out, e.g. **the floor was cleaned**

relative clause   a special type of subordinate clause that makes the meaning of a noun more specific by using a pronoun to link back to the noun

relative pronoun   we use relative pronouns **after** a noun, to make it clear which person or thing we are talking about, or in relative clauses, to tell us more about a person or thing, e.g. **who**, **which**, **that**, **who(m)**, **whose**

semicolon   a punctuation mark to show a break that is stronger than a comma but not as final as a full stop. It's used between two main clauses that balance each other and are closely linked. You can also use a semicolon as a stronger division in a sentence or list that already contains commas

subject   the subject of a sentence is generally the person or thing that the sentence is about, often the person or thing that performs the action of a verb

synonym   a word or phrase that means exactly or nearly the same as another word or phrase in the same language

Punctuation chart

Punctuation mark word	Symbol	Note	Example
apostrophe	'	Can show that something belongs to someone or something Can show that letters are missed out	the girl's hat the girls' hats can't cannot she'd she would/she had
brackets	(....)	Can be used to show that a word or phrase has been added	We said thank you (but we didn't mean it really!).
bullet point	•	Can be used to make a list clear	Things to buy: • sausages • bananas • baked beans
colon	:	Can be used before you make a list Can be used to give more examples after the first part of a sentence	See above The dogs are very funny: they are trained to do tricks.
comma	,	Can make a sentence clear or change the meaning of the sentence To separate the items in a list	Slow children running Slow, children running I like sausages, bananas and baked beans.
dash	–	Can be used to add a bit more information to a sentence It's informal	The dogs are very funny – the old brown one makes me laugh.
full stop	.	Can be used at the end of a sentence to show it has finished It also shows that a word is shortened or contracted	I went to the dog show. On the 23rd of Sept. I went to the dog show.

Handy hints

Top tips on spelling

1) Try using your phonics knowledge first.

2) Does it look right? If not, what changes would make sense?

3) Use analogy: do you know another word that sounds similar and that you could use as a starting point, e.g. if it's **baby/babies**, then it's probably going to be **city/cities**.

4) If it's a long word, say the syllables; write each syllable as a chunk

5) Use morphology: think about the root word and then about whether the word might have a prefix or a suffix that might help you to spell it, e.g. **medical** and **medicine**.

6) Use etymology: think about a word's history and, in particular, its origins in earlier forms of English or other languages to see if that might help you to spell it, e.g. **circumference** from the Latin *circumferentia* meaning the line around a circle.

7) Don't always rely on the spellcheck when working on the computer – keep thinking for yourself so that when you are writing away from technology or on your own, you don't get stuck.

accommodate	curiosity	interfere	restaurant
according	desperate	language	rhythm
aggressive	develop	lightning	secretary
ancient	disastrous	mischievous	sincere(ly)
appreciate	environment	necessary	stomach
available	especially	nuisance	suggest
awkward	excellent	occur	system
bruise	explanation	parliament	thorough
cemetery	foreign	physical	variety
communicate	frequently	privilege	vehicle
competition	guarantee	programme	
conscious	hindrance	queue	
correspond	immediate(ly)	recommend	

Presentation

Six tips on handwriting

1) Space out letters, words and sentences evenly.

2) Keep the size of your letters even.

3) Write on the lines if you are writing on lined paper or keep straight if you are not.

4) Make sure that your pen or pencil is comfortable (and that the pencil is sharp).

5) Use an eraser (rubber, correction fluid or correction pen) if you make a mistake.

6) If **you** can't read it then the chances are that neither can anyone else. Keep it neat all the time.

Rules for capital letters

Use capital letters for:

- people's names
- people's titles (like **Mrs** Jones)
- places
- days of the week
- months of the year
- organisations.

Full stops

Always put a full stop at the end of a sentence unless you are using a **?** or a **!**

My part of East London has a character all its own. There is a collection of streets, parallel to each other, leading back from the old railway line .

The crumbling terraced houses are full of life, even if they look old. Above them are the Docklands Light Railway lines.

Huge concrete pillars hold up these tracks. They remind me of enormous grey legs striding across the city.

The driverless trains on them are like blue caterpillars crawling slowly on their way to find somewhere to rest underneath the railway arches.

These arches make a new little world. In between the pillars, the spaces have been cleverly used. Some spaces have been bricked in and walls divide them into workshops or dark offices.

Rising Stars UK Ltd, 7 Hatchers Mews, Bermondsey Street, London SE1 3GS

www.risingstars-uk.com

Acknowledgements

Page 22 – Adapted from *Shooting the Elephant* by George Orwell. Copyright © George Orwell, 1946. Reprinted by permission of Houghton Mifflin Harcourt Publishing Company and Bill Hamilton as the Literary Executor of the Estate of the Late Sonia Brownell Orwell

Page 26 – William Shakespeare, ROMEO AND JULIET, edited by Philip Page and Marilyn Petit. Shakespeare Graphics (Hodder Murray, 1999), illustrations © 1999 by Philip Page. Reproduced in adaption form by permission of the illustrator and Hodder Education

Page 28 – Extract from *Little House in the Big Woods* by Laura Ingalls Wilder, Methuen Children's Books. Reprinted by permission of HarperCollins Publishers Ltd.

Page 34 – Extract from *Warrior Scarlet* by Rosemary Sutcliff, published by Oxford University Press and Puffin. Reprinted with permission of David Higham Associates

Page 38 – Extract from *Hannah Goslar Remembers* by Alison Leslie Gold. © Alison Leslie Gold, 1998. Published by Bloomsbury

Page 40 – Extract from *Ziata's Diary: A Child's Life in Sarajevo* by Zlata Filipovic, translated by Christina Pribichevich-Zoric (Viking 1994, first published in France as 'Le Journal de Zlata' by Fixot et editions Robert Laffont 1993). Copyright © Fixot et editions Robert Laffont 1993. Reproduced by permission of Penguin Books Ltd.

Page 42 – 'Boo!' by Kevin Crossley-Holland from *Short! A Book of Very Short Stories* (OUP, 1998), copyright © Kevin Crossely-Holland 1998, reprinted with permission of Oxford University Press

Page 48 – Extract from *Cider with Rosie* by Laurie Lee, published by The Hogarth Press. Reprinted by permission of The Random House Group Ltd and Curtis Brown Group Ltd, London, on behalf of the estate of Laurie Lee. Copyright © Laurie Lee 1959

Page 50 – Extract from 'The Kangeroo's Coff' by Anthony Twaite, from *Allsorts of Poems,* Angus and Robertson 1978

Page 56 – Extract from *The Machine*. Copyright © Robert Westall 1975. First published by Macmillan Children's Books 1975

Every effort has been made to trace copyright holders and obtain their permission for the use of copyright materials. The authors and publisher will gladly receive information enabling them to rectify any error or omission in subsequent editions.

All facts are correct at the time of going to press.

Published 2013

Text, design and layout © Rising Stars UK Ltd.

Authors: Les Ray and Gill Budgell

Educational consultant: Shareen Mayers, Routes to Success, Sutton

Text design: Green Desert Ltd

Cover design: West 8 Design

Illustrations: HL Studios

Publisher: Camilla Erskine

Copy Editor: Sarah Davies

British Library Cataloguing in Publication Data.

A CIP record for this book is available from the British Library.

ISBN: 978-0-85769-681-6

Printed by Craft Print International Ltd, Singapore